A BRAND-NEW YEAR—
A PROMISING NEW START

With expert readings and forecasts, you can chart a course to romance, adventure, good health, or career opportunities while gaining valuable insight into yourself and others. Offering a daily outlook for 18 full months, this fascinating guide shows you:

- The important dates in your life
- What to expect from an astrological reading
- How the stars can help you stay healthy and fit
  And more!

Let this sound advice guide you through a year of heavenly possibilities—for today and for every day of 2014!

SYDNEY OMARR'S® DAY-BY-DAY ASTROLOGICAL GUIDE FOR

ARIES—March 21–April 19
TAURUS—April 20–May 20
GEMINI—May 21–June 20
CANCER—June 21–July 22
LEO—July 23–August 22
VIRGO—August 23–September 22
LIBRA—September 23–October 22
SCORPIO—October 23–November 21
SAGITTARIUS—November 22–December 21
CAPRICORN—December 22–January 19
AQUARIUS—January 20–February 18
PISCES—February 19–March 20

IN 2014

SYDNEY OMARR'S®

DAY-BY-DAY ASTROLOGICAL GUIDE FOR

CANCER

JUNE 21–JULY 22

2014

by Trish MacGregor
with Rob MacGregor

A SIGNET BOOK

SIGNET
Published by the Penguin Group
Penguin Group (USA) Inc., 375 Hudson Street,
New York, New York 10014, USA

USA / Canada / UK / Ireland / Australia / New Zealand / India / South Africa / China

Penguin Books Ltd., Registered Offices: 80 Strand, London WC2R 0RL, England
For more information about the Penguin Group visit penguin.com.

First published by Signet, an imprint of New American Library,
a division of Penguin Group (USA) Inc.

First Printing, June 2013

Sydney Omarr's is a registered trademark of Writers House, LLC.

Sydney Omarr® is syndicated worldwide by Los Angeles Times Syndicate.

REGISTERED TRADEMARK—MARCA REGISTRADA

ISBN 978-0-451-41389-5

Printed in the United States of America
10 9 8 7 6 5 4 3 2 1

ALWAYS LEARNING   PEARSON

CONTENTS

CHAPTER 1

The New You

We branded 2012 the year of the paradigm shift, and since the world didn't end, 2013 became the year of transformation. Now here you are at the doorstep of 2014, and the person who steps through is the new you!

And who is this new you likely to be? For some clues, let's take a look at the transits of the outer planets this year. These planets exert the most influence over our daily lives because they take so long to move through a single sign. Pluto, for instance, entered Capricorn in 2008 and won't leave until early 2024. Neptune, which takes about fourteen years to move through a sign, entered Pisces in early February 2012 and will be there until late January 2026. Uranus entered Aries in March 2011 and leaves that sign in March 2019. So just these three planets exert a powerful influence over a number of years.

The next two planets that influence us over a period of time are Saturn, which takes two and a half years to transit a sign, and Jupiter, which usually takes about a year. Each of these planets is covered extensively in various parts of the book, and each one has its role in the formation of the new you in 2014.

In the next chapter we talk about what each of the planets represents, what signs they rule, and just about anything else you could ever want to know about them astrologically. In a later chapter historical perspectives are provided on the three slowest-moving planets. But this chapter let's take an in-depth look at the planet Uranus and how its energies will help define the new you.

Uranus

This planet symbolizes revolution, genius, rebellion, earthquakes, sudden, unexpected events and change, our individuality, inventions and discoveries, electricity, radio, TV, electronics, lightning. You get the idea. Its energy isn't the least bit subtle. It sweeps into our lives, stirs up mass movements, and knocks down the old to make way for the new.

On March 11, 2011, the day that Uranus entered Aries, there was a 9.0 earthquake near the east coast of Honshu, Japan. The quake triggered a twenty-three-foot tsunami that hammered Japan's coast and caused an explosion at the Fukushima nuclear plant and the subsequent worst nuclear disaster since Chernobyl twenty-five years ago.

Any country would be devastated by just one of these events. But to have all three within twenty-four hours resulted in some staggering statistics. According to an earthquake report issued by http://earthquake-report.com, about twenty thousand people are either dead or missing; more than a million buildings were destroyed, eighty thousand residents were evacuated from a twelve-mile radius around the plant, and the economic losses range from between $100 to $500 billion, most of it created within seventy minutes.

As of late 2011 the evacuees have still not been permitted to go home, and the authorities are still cooling down the plant. The environmental ministry in Japan says an area of 930 square mi is affected.

All of these events are right in line with the archetypal energy of Uranus transiting Aries, the warrior.

Other facets of this transit are revolution and rebellion. First there were the uprisings in the Arab world in late 2010 that swept three leaders out of power—the heads of Tunisia, Egypt, and Libya. Then in September 2011 came a grassroots protest: Occupy Wall Street. On September 17 about two thousand people congregated in downtown Manhattan and marched up Broadway. En route they stopped at Zuccotti Park and more than a hundred of the protesters stayed the night and set up an encampment.

The mainstream media ignored the protest at first. Then Keith Olbermann, on Current TV, started covering it, and suddenly so did everyone else. From the Occupy Web site: ". . . we kicked off a protest against bank bailouts, corporate greed, and the unchecked power of Wall Street in Washington." The movement rapidly gained global support, and by its one-month anniversary had spread to eighty-two countries.

It takes eighty-four years for Uranus to move through the zodiac. So let's take a trip down memory lane to the last time Uranus transited the sign of Aries. In mid-January 1928 Uranus entered Aries and remained there until late March 1935. Here are some of the events that occurred during this period:

- First air-conditioned office opens in the U.S. in San Antonio
- Scotch tape first marketed by 3M company
- First trans-Atlantic TV image received
- Amelia Earhart first woman to fly the Atlantic— as a passenger
- Alexander Fleming discovers penicillin
- Yo-yo introduced
- First regularly scheduled TV is broadcast three nights a week
- German airship *Graf Zeppelin* begins a round-the-world flight
- Stock market crash
- Salvador Dali's first one-man show
- Bingo invented
- Planet Pluto named
- Hostess Twinkies invented
- N.Y. Yankee Babe Ruth hits three consecutive homers
- First nudist colony opens
- First radar detection of planes
- *N.Y. World* reports disappearance of supreme court justice Joseph Crater
- N.Y.C. College offers first course in radio advertising
- A bloodless coup d'état in Brazil
- First *Dracula* movie released
- Empire State Building opens in N.Y.C.
- Al Capone is indicted on 5,000 counts of prohibition and perjury

- Babe Ruth hits his 600th home run
- Alka Seltzer goes on sale
- Jane Addams—first U.S. woman named corecipient of Nobel Peace Prize
- Martial law is declared in Honduras to stop revolt by banana workers fired by United Fruit
- El Salvador army kills four thousand protesting farmers
- First patent issued for a tree, to James Markham for a peach tree
- Amelia Earhart is first woman to fly solo across the Atlantic
- Yellow fever vaccine for humans announced
- U.S. federal gas tax enacted
- Earthquake kills seventy thousand in Kansu, China
- Hitler proclaims end of Marxism
- Bank holidays declared in six states to prevent run on banks
- F.D.R. inaugurated as thirty-second pres, pledges to pull U.S. out of Depression and says, "We have nothing to fear but fear itself."
- F.D.R. proclaims ten-day bank holiday
- Dachau, first concentration camp, completed
- First flight over Mount Everest
- Nazis stage public book burnings in Germany
- Loch Ness Monster is first reported
- German Secret State Police (Gestapo) established
- In London five hundred thousand march against anti-Semitism
- Alcatraz officially becomes a federal prison
- *Flash Gordon* comic strip debuts

- F.D.R. signs Home Owners Loan Act
- First Sugar Bowl and first Orange Bowl
- First canned beer is sold
- Monopoly is invented
- First Penguin book is published
- Four hundred thousand demonstrators against fascism in Madrid
- *Billboard* magazine publishes its first music Hit Parade
- The first stock car race is held in Daytona Beach, Florida
- *Gone With the Wind* by Margaret Mitchell is published
- Spanish Civil War begins; General Francisco Franco leads uprising
- King Edward VIII abdicates throne to marry Mrs. Wallis Simpson

This list represents just a small sampling of the thousands of events that occurred during Uranus' last transit of Aries. But as you read through this list you undoubtedly see a pattern—war, rebellion, uprisings, numerous discoveries and many "firsts," the rise of Hitler and Nazi Germany, natural disasters like earthquakes, the completion of engineering marvels like the Empire State Building and Hoover Dam, the precipitous drop of the stock market and the depression that followed.

Aries is not only the sign of the warrior, but of the entrepreneur, the trailblazer, the one who is so independent and forward thinking that he marches to a different drummer. Aries is fearless, a risk-taker, and like the *Star Trek* motto, goes where no man (or woman) has gone before. So when you combine Aries with the planet that symbolizes all the traits mentioned earlier, you have an intriguing MO for the emergence of the new you.

The new you will be emerging into a new planetary environment, so let's start there.

Innovations

Book publishing. Once the dust settles, the book publishing industry and retail bookstores in general will be vastly changed from the way they have existed for years. The emergence of the eBook, the Kindle, Nook, and other electronic reading devices is, as of this writing in early 2012, creating chaos. With the bankruptcy of Borders Books, Barnes & Noble is the only game left in town, the largest book retailer in the U.S., and they don't stock every book that is published. So what happens to a book when Barnes & Noble doesn't carry it? That depends.

If the book is an eBook that sells for a fraction of the price of a hardback book—$9.99 versus, say, $25 or $30—perhaps the lack of hardcover sales are compensated for because more people can afford to buy an eBook than a hardcover. A young woman in Minnesota wrote a romance novel that was rejected by major publishers, so she self-published the novel as an eBook, sold it for $2.99, and sold millions of copies. Within a year she paid a million cash for her first home.

So what might we expect this year? Perhaps the publishing and bookstore industry are learning that life is interconnected. Ebooks, after all, save trees. Saving trees helps the environment. Helping the environment aids the planet. So perhaps by the time this transit is finished ebooks will be the norm, and only libraries will carry print books.

Another possible repercussion is that more authors will self-publish in ebooks. With the advent of blogs and online software that makes building a Web site easier than a few years ago, there may come a time when authors charge for access to their blogs, where entire novels and books are written.

More social media. MySpace, Facebook, Twitter, LinkedIn, Google Friends ... before Uranus leaves Aries, expect more social media to surface. Uranus rules the Internet, so the Internet itself may evolve and change in important ways before the end of this transit.

Medical breakthroughs. During Uranus' last transit of Aries, the medical breakthroughs were significant: treatment for yellow fever, development of penicillin, anesthesia, insulin shock therapy, vitamin B3, and protonsil, the first sulphur drug, which was used to treat infections caused by streptococcus. So this time around we can expect other types of breakthroughs in medicine, health, and pharmacology. A cure for AIDS? Cancer? Heart disease?

Rebellion/revolution. More planetary changes are likely, and so is continued rebellion by the 99 percent. The us-versus-them mentality has brought about a wider gap between rich and poor, with the middle class fading rapidly. Groups of urban survivalists have sprung up, some of them extremists.

The U.S., with the most powerful military in the world (which also eats up the largest chunk of the federal budget), continues to police the rest of the planet, while pushing the needs of its own citizens into a dark hole labeled *later*.

The contentiousness of the political divide in the U.S. was glaringly obvious in the health care debate that raged in early 2011 and later that year in the debt crisis debates. These trends, unfortunately, may get worse before Uranus leaves Aries.

However, if we remember that Uranus' job is to shake up the status quo so that new paradigms, new ways of doing things, can be born, then we could see the birth of new political parties that emphasize peace over war. Perhaps we'll see a complete withdrawal of U.S. troops from the Mideast.

Politics. The warrior archetype is certainly prevalent these days in politics. As a new paradigm is being birthed, the old paradigm isn't dying an easy death.

The meltdown in 2008 resulted in massive bailouts to banks, the collapse of institutions, and billions of stimulus dollars poured into the economy. It was the Obama administration's equivalent of F.D.R.'s New Deal, passed during his first term in response to the Great Depression. During this period Social Security was implemented.

As Uranus continues its transit through Aries, we may see the implementation of new social or economic programs that aid people rather than banks and corporations. It's doubtful we'll see any true universal health coverage, at least not if the past is any indication. But *if* a visionary was swept into the White House in 2016, *if* the corporate greed has been overturned, *if* Wall Street is regulated and the entire banking system overhauled, then maybe. But it's a lot of *if*s.

Discoveries. Numerous discoveries and inventions came about during Uranus's last pass through Aries. This transit could produce the twenty-first–century equivalents in technology, television, the Internet, health and medicine, engineering, movies, earthquake detection, music, ebooks, alternative fuels.

World records. During Uranus' last transit of Aries many "firsts" occurred, and world records were set. This time around we could see more of the same—in space flight, cars that run on alternative fuels, high-speed trains, athletics, even the ways our homes and office buildings are powered. The world may go green more quickly than we can imagine.

With Uranus, we either embrace change—or it's forced upon us. So let's take a look at how each of us can embrace the change Uranus is ushering into our personal lives.

Aries ♈

Cardinal Fire Sign

The new you is likely to be an improved version of the old you. The things you disliked about yourself a few years ago will fall away. Maybe a belief system you clung to a few years back was no longer serving your best interests and has now shattered, and you're casting about for new beliefs, new ways of being. Or perhaps a significant relationship has fallen apart. Or you lost your job. In whatever area your life was sterile and routine, Uranus has shaken things up.

As an Aries, you're probably well aware of where your life is stale and routine and do your best to turn it around. That means you're ahead of the game, and the Uranus transit through your sign will be exciting. But in the event you're the rare Aries who doesn't mind routine, this transit will be jarring, and the new you will emerge from the shock. Uranus has been in Aries for about three years now, so you should have a fairly clear idea how the transit is affecting you.

The best way for you to navigate this transit is to do what you do naturally: maintain a sense of adventure about life; be passionate in all that you undertake; keep your steady focus, don't hesitate to explore. In addition treat others the way you like to be treated. In love relationships strive to be more cooperative, to see things the way your partner does. In your career, with your creative work, complete what you start.

Unusual ideas and idiosyncratic individuals are part of this transit package. You won't be bored, but be careful that life doesn't become just one adrenaline high after the other. Welcome change, embrace it, even if it's thrust on you.

Taurus ♉
Fixed Earth Sign

Unless you have some planets in fire signs, you probably won't like this transit very much. It jars your grounded, Taurean sensibilities. However, because you're the most stubborn, resilient, and resolute sign in the zodiac, you come through it intact, with a new you to show to the world.

The new you in 2014 may be less stubborn, for one thing. The Uranus transit, after all, occurs in your solar twelfth house, so a lot of *stuff* is being stirred up in your unconscious. You may discover power you have disowned over the years and take it back. Or you may discover your dreams are filled with insights and information that aid you. Ideas that come to you during this transit are likely to be unusual, and it will be up to that grounded side of your personality to translate them into something useful.

As a fixed earth sign, you like things in your life to be orderly, practical, even predictable. You're slow to change your opinions and beliefs. *Stability* is your middle name. Since this transit occurs in your solar twelfth house, Uranus shakes up your world from the inside out. Your greatest strength during this period is to tackle one issue at a time and deal with it the way you do everything else in your life—carefully, thoroughly, meticulously.

The new you who emerges this year is the Taurus who has tackled these issues and reclaimed personal power and is ready to embrace everything that comes your way.

Gemini ♊

Mutable Air Sign

The new you who emerges in 2014 is likely to be more focused, ready to implement all the unusual ideas that are flowing through you. The way you implement these ideas, of course, is through your communication skills and by using your flexibility to quickly adapt to new situations.

Uranus forms a beneficial angle to your sun during

this transit, which enhances your innate abilities and attracts unusual people, excitement, and abrupt, positive change. It occurs in your solar eleventh house of friends, wishes, and dreams. The new you is apt to be more involved in a group—a theater group, writing, bridge, esoteric—that supports your interests and passions. In some way this group helps you to achieve your wishes and dreams.

New opportunities should surface for self-expression. If you've always had a secret yearning to write a novel or screenplay, for example, this transit helps you to do it. If you're an amateur photographer, you may have an opportunity to become a professional. The transit will free you from limiting circumstances—a relationship that no longer works, a job that has grown stale and predictable, a career that no longer feels right. Your comfortable ruts will become history.

Cancer ♋
Cardinal Water Sign

In 2014 the new you is a career-oriented individual. The Uranus transit through Aries forms a challenging angle to your sun and occurs in your tenth house of career, so you've probably experienced or are experiencing radical, abrupt professional changes. Your job, for example, could be outsourced. Or you get a new boss whom you don't like. Or you have to take a cut in pay. Whatever the curve ball that Uranus in Aries throws your way, Cancer, regard it as an opportunity, and watch the new you begin to take shape.

The new you will be able to draw steadily upon the

vast reservoir of your intuition, will gain immeasurably from insights and information gleaned from your dreams, and will be readily able to put these insights to work.

The lens through which you see the world is personal, subjective, emotional. Your nurturing and intuitive abilities are your greatest strengths and will serve the new you even better than they served the former you! You eagerly seek out the new and different and embrace change.

Leo ♌

Fixed Fire Sign

The new you who emerges from this transit will have vastly improved skills and talents and less ego. Uranus forms a beneficial angle to your sun during this transit and bolsters all the qualities for which you're known and loved—your warmth, compassion, flair for drama, and ability to make friends with just about anyone.

The sudden, exciting changes that are brought about prompt you to try new forms of self-expression. Your creative drive soars. The stimulating people you encounter during this transit, individuals who may be geniuses in their fields, may prove helpful to you in some way. There could be romance and love with this transit too, Leo. So many intriguing individuals are entering your life now that you'll have your pick!

The new you may undertake a spiritual quest of some kind and travel abroad in search of esoteric knowledge. Or you may go to college, grad school, or law school. You will make time to keep yourself fit and healthy through a regular fitness regimen.

Virgo ♍
Mutable Earth Sign

This transit forms a challenging angle to your sun sign and is shaking up those areas that have become routine in your life. The new you who emerges this year will still be a perfectionist who is precise and detailed oriented, but no longer to the point of obsession.

The transit occurs in your solar eighth house—shared resources. Since the eighth house represents joint resources, your partner's income may rise or fall suddenly or unexpectedly. You could inherit money. It's an excellent time to get out of debt. In fact, debt may be another limitation that you find intolerable. The new you will probably be more frugal, paying for things in cash.

Any new romance that comes your way could be highly sexual and have a deeply intuitive component to it.

Libra ♎
Cardinal Air Sign

The new you who emerges in 2014 will still possess all the wonderful qualities that make you the person so many people love. You will still be able to put yourself in someone else's shoes and see the world through the eyes of another. But you aren't as likely to bend over backward to please other people, and finding peace and harmony won't be as difficult as it may have been in the past.

The new you will reach out to people more readily. The social grace with which you do this will enable you to win over the opposition every time. This transit occurs in your solar seventh house of partnerships. Both romantic and business partnerships could be challenged during this transit, but you ride the tide, whatever it is, and learn from the experiences. When sudden, unexpected events bring about the beginning and end of partnerships, you stand up for who you are and what you really believe, and in doing so you break free of restrictions that have become unbearable.

This transit may seem harsh at times. It appears that stuff is happening *to* you, that the universe is ganging up against you. But what's actually happening is that energies you have repressed over the years are now scrambling for release. Any relationship that ends under this transit—through death or otherwise—does so because it has served its purpose. Relationships that begin during this transit are apt to be exciting, different in some way, and stimulating mentally, emotionally, and spiritually.

Go with the flow, Libra. That's the new you.

Scorpio ♏

Fixed Water Sign

The new you who emerges in 2014 is influenced by several factors—Uranus in Aries, certainly, but also by

Saturn transiting your sign, something we'll talk about in a later chapter. This new you will be more intuitive and less stubborn and perhaps less secretive as well. You will continue to delve deeply for answers, but in a less obsessive way. You won't be doing it with a feeling that it must be done immediately. Tomorrow or next week will work fine too.

This transit is about freedom—from restrictions and limitations in any area of your life that prevent you from evolving creatively, spiritually, or emotionally. As a fixed water sign, you probably don't like change any more than your fixed-sign brothers—Taurus, Leo, and Aquarius. But change you must. It's easier if you can learn to embrace change rather than resist it so that change isn't thrust on you, and that's what the new you achieves!

Since this transit occurs in your solar sixth house, the area most likely to be impacted is your daily work routine and health. The possible scenarios depend on how rigid, routine, or boring your daily work is; whether you stick to this work primarily because it's comfortable; and whether or not you enjoy what you're doing. The health aspect depends on how well you take care of yourself and your beliefs about health. In other words, if you believe that people get colds every winter, you probably will get a cold every winter. So take inventory of your beliefs, Scorpio. The new, emerging you has a clear handle on his or her beliefs.

Sagittarius ♐
Mutable Fire Sign

The new you who emerges from this Uranus transit, Sagittarius, is as exciting and adventurous as always, but with some important changes. You're now ready to actually be in a romantic partnership, to communicate honestly with your partner, to give for the joy of giving. It's likely that romantic relationships begin and end suddenly and your creativity is taking you in new directions. The new you is fine with whatever is happening. You eagerly embrace the changes in your life.

With Uranus in Aries forming a beneficial angle to your sun, you're able to become who you really are; it's much easier to reshape your personality. Your creative self-expression shines forth, and new venues for creativity open up. You may find yourself involved in creative projects that are totally different from anything you've done before, that prompt you to stretch your creativity in new ways.

If you're a Sadge who enjoys travel—and you probably are, many of your sign do—you'll be doing more of it during this transit. In fact, abundant foreign travel may be an intricate part of the new you.

Capricorn ♑
Cardinal Earth Sign

The new you who emerges in 2014 will be just as focused as you usually are, but with less of an obsessive edge. You're not obsessive the way a Scorpio is, for instance, but there can be an intensity about your focus that doesn't serve your best interests. Your ability to plow through any obstacle you encounter will enable you to break free of any limitations and restrictions that are either self-imposed or imposed on you by others. The new you will have better methods for doing this.

The transit occurs in your solar fourth house—your domestic environment—so let's take a look at some possible scenarios:

Your parents move in with you.

Your employer is relocating, and if you want to keep your job, you have to move too.

Your partner or spouse is laid off at work, and you have to sell your home and move to a smaller place.

Your parents get divorced, and you have to relocate.

The fourth house represents the foundation of your life, the most intimate and personal part of who you are. For most of us, changes in this area can be deeply unsettling. Any part of this area that has grown stale, rigid, or routine will be affected. But if your home life is vibrant and exciting, then it won't be impacted.

The new you will strive to be more flexible and will be better equipped to go with the flow emotionally, creatively, and spiritually.

Aquarius ≈

Fixed Air Sign

The new you who emerges this year will be edgier and more idiosyncratic, with more unusual ideas. The Uranus transit through Aries forms a beneficial angle to your sun and occurs in your solar third house, which represents communication, your conscious mind, neighborhood and neighbors, siblings, daily life, and travel. This area is where you're apt to experience all the excitement of this transit—and the place from which the new you emerges.

The new you is excited by the exploration of consciousness and how it molds and shapes our perceptions, and how, in fact, it may attract the kinds of experiences we have. During this transit your consciousness is expanding, leaping outward, seeking new ideas, and exploring different belief systems and lifestyles. You may move quite suddenly and unexpectedly, but it turns out to be beneficial for you. You may undertake creative projects that are outside your usual talents and abilities and discover a new facet of your personality. This period is all about trying the new and unexplored, adventures in consciousness and communication.

The new you knows it's the ideal time to start a blog, build a Web site, or write a novel or book and gets involved with community activities. Uranus, the planet that rules your sign, won't disappoint you during this transit.

Pisces ♓
Mutable Water Sign

The new you who emerges this year is just as imaginative and intuitive as always but less conflicted, so it's easier for you to make decisions. Like your mutable siblings—Gemini, Virgo, and Sagittarius—you don't have any problem with change. But because this transit occurs in a fire sign, Aries, your solar second house of finances, this is the area where the new you is likely to emerge.

The new you will insist on working in a profession or career that is in line with your deeper beliefs and ideals. The new you will follow intuitive leads, network with others of like mind, and strive to turn any challenge into a blessing. You'll understand that nothing is too wild to try, too *out there* to consider. The new you will understand the wisdom of financial prudence, will pay cash for everything, and probably cut up the credit cards too.

Astrological Basics

On the day you were born, what was the weather like? If you were born at night, had the moon already risen? Was it full or the shape of a Cheshire cat's grin? Was the delivery ward quiet or bustling with activity? Unless your mom or dad has a very good memory, you'll probably never know the full details. But there's one thing you can know for sure: on the day you were born the sun was located in a particular zone of the zodiac, an imaginary 360-degree belt that circles the earth. The belt is divided into twelve 30-degree portions called signs.

If you were born between July 23 and August 22, the sun was passing through the sign of Leo, so we say that your sun sign is Leo. Each of the twelve signs has distinct attributes and characteristics. Leos, for instance, love being the center of attention. They're warm, compassionate people with a flair for the dramatic. Virgos, born between August 23 and September 22, are perfectionists with discriminating intellects and a genius for details. Capricorns, born between

December 22 and January 19, are the worker bees of the zodiac, serious minded, ambitious, industrious.

How Signs Are Classified

As you probably gathered from the first chapter, the twelve signs are categorized according to element and quality or modality. The first category, element, reads like a basic science lesson—fire, earth, air, and water—and describes the general physical characteristics of the signs.

Fire signs—Aries, Leo, Sagittarius—are warm, dynamic individuals who are always passionate about what they do.

Earth signs—Taurus, Virgo, Capricorn—are the builders of the zodiac, practical and efficient, grounded in everything they do.

Air signs—Gemini, Libra, Aquarius—are people who live mostly in the world of ideas. They are terrific communicators.

Water signs—Cancer, Scorpio, Pisces—live through their emotions, imaginations, and intuitions.

The second category describes how each sign operates in the physical world, how adaptable it is to circumstances:

Cardinal signs—Aries, Cancer, Libra, Capricorn—are initiators. These people are active, impatient, restless. They're great at starting things, but unless a project or a relationship holds their attention, they lose interest and may not finish what they start.

Fixed signs—Taurus, Leo, Scorpio, Aquarius—are deliberate, controlled, resolute. These individuals tend to move more slowly than cardinal signs, are often stubborn, and resist change. They seek roots and stability and are always in the game for the long haul. They aren't quitters.

Mutable signs—Gemini, Virgo, Sagittarius, Pisces—are adaptable. These people are flexible, changeable, communicative. They don't get locked into rigid patterns or belief systems.

TABLE 1 SUN SIGNS

Sign	Date	Element	Quality
Aries ♈	March 21–April 19	Fire	Cardinal
Taurus ♉	April 20–May 20	Earth	Fixed
Gemini ♊	May 21–June 21	Air	Mutable
Cancer ♋	June 22–July 22	Water	Cardinal
Leo ♌	July 23–August 22	Fire	Fixed
Virgo ♍	August 23–September 22	Earth	Mutable
Libra ♎	September 23–October 22	Air	Cardinal
Scorpio ♏	October 23–November 21	Water	Fixed
Sagittarius ♐	November 22–December 21	Fire	Mutable
Capricorn ♑	December 22–January 19	Earth	Cardinal
Aquarius ♒	January 20–February 18	Air	Fixed
Pisces ♓	February 19–March 20	Water	Mutable

The Planets

The planets in astrology are the players who make things happen. They're the characters in the story of your life. This story always begins with the sun, the giver of life.

Your sun sign describes your self-expression, your primal energy, the essence of who you are. It's the archetypal pattern of your Self. When you know another person's sun sign, you already have a great deal of information about that person. Let's say you're a Taurus who has just started dating a Gemini. How compatible are you?

On the surface, it wouldn't seem that you have much in common. Taurus is a fixed earth sign; Gemini is a mutable air sign. Taurus is persistent, stubborn, practical, a cultivator as opposed to an initiator. Gemini is a chameleon, a communicator, social, with a mind as quick as lightning. Taurus is ruled by Venus, which governs the arts, money, beauty, love, and romance, and Gemini is ruled by Mercury, which governs communication and travel. There doesn't seem to be much common ground. But before we write off this combination, let's look a little deeper.

Suppose the Taurus has Mercury in Gemini, and suppose the Gemini has Venus in Taurus? This would mean that the Taurus and Gemini each have their rulers in the other person's sign. They probably communicate well and enjoy travel and books (Mercury) and would see eye to eye on romance, art, and music (Venus). They might get along so well, in fact, that they collaborate on creative projects.

Each of us is also influenced by the other nine planets (the sun and moon are treated like planets in astrology) and the signs they were transiting when you were born. Suppose our Taurus and Gemini have the same moon sign? The moon rules our inner needs, emotions and intuition, and all that makes us feel secure within ourselves. Quite often compatible moon signs can overcome even the most glaring difference in sun signs because the two people share similar emotions.

In the sections on predictions your sun sign always takes center stage, and every prediction is based on the movement of the transiting planets in relation to your sun sign. Let's say you're a Sagittarius. Between November 16 and December 11 this year Venus will be transiting your sign. What's this mean for you? Well, since Venus rules—among other things—romance, you can expect your love life to pick up significantly during these weeks. Other people will find you attractive and be more open to your ideas, and you'll radiate a certain charisma. Your creative endeavors will move full steam ahead.

Table 2 provides an overview of the planets and the signs that they rule. Keep in mind that the moon is the swiftest-moving planet, changing signs about every two and a half days, and that Pluto is the snail of the zodiac, taking as long as thirty years to transit a single sign. Although the faster-moving planets—the moon, Mercury, Venus, and Mars—have an impact on our lives, it's the slow pokes—Uranus, Neptune, and Pluto—that bring about the most profound influence and change. Jupiter and Saturn fall between the others in terms of speed. This year Jupiter spends the first six months in Cancer, then enters Leo on July 16 and doesn't leave that sign until August 11, 2015.

In the section on predictions the most frequent references are to the transits of Mercury, Venus, and Mars and the movements of the transiting moon.

Now glance through Table 2. When a sign is in parentheses, it means the planet corules that sign. This assignation dates back to when we thought there were only seven planets in the solar system. But since there were still twelve signs, some of the planets had to do double duty!

TABLE 2 THE PLANETS

Planet	Rules	Attributes of Planet
Sun ☉	Leo	Self-expression, primal energy, creative ability, ego, individuality
Moon ☽	Cancer	Emotions, intuition, mother or wife, security
Mercury ☿	Gemini, Virgo	Intellect, mental acuity, communication, logic, reasoning, travel, contracts
Venus ♀	Taurus, Libra	Love, romance, beauty, artistic instincts, the arts, music, material and financial resources
Mars ♂	Aries (Scorpio)	Physical and sexual energy, aggression, drive
Jupiter ♃	Sagittarius (Pisces)	Luck, expansion, success, prosperity, growth, creativity, spiritual interests, higher education, law
Saturn ♄	Capricorn (Aquarius)	Laws of physical universe, discipline, responsibility, structure, karma, authority
Uranus ♅	Aquarius	Individuality, genius, eccentricity, originality, science, revolution

Planet	Rules	Attributes of Planet
Neptune ♆	Pisces	Visionary self, illusions, what's hidden, psychic ability, dissolution of ego boundaries, spiritual insights, dreams
Pluto ♀ ♇	Scorpio	The darker side, death, sex, regeneration, rebirth, profound and permanent change, transformation

Houses and Rising Signs

In the instant you drew your first breath, one of the signs of the zodiac was just passing over the eastern horizon. Astrologers refer to this as the rising sign or ascendant. It's what makes your horoscope unique. Think of your ascendant as the front door of your horoscope, the place where you enter into this life and begin your journey.

Your ascendant is based on the exact moment of your birth, and the other signs follow counterclockwise. If you have Taurus rising, for example, that is the cusp of your first house. The cusp of the second would be Gemini, of the third Cancer, and so on around the horoscope circle in a counterclockwise direction. Each house governs a particular area of life, which is outlined below.

The best way to find out your rising sign is to have your horoscope drawn up by an astrologer. For those of you with access to the Internet, though, there are several sites that provide free birth horoscopes: www

.astro.com and www.cafeastrology.com are two good ones.

In a horoscope the ascendant (cusp of the first house), IC (cusp of the fourth house), descendant (cusp of the seventh house) and MC (cusp of the tenth house) are considered to be the most critical angles. Any planets that fall close to these angles are extremely important in the overall astrological picture of who you are. By the same token, planets that fall in the first, fourth, seventh, and tenth houses are also considered to be important.

Now here's a rundown on what the houses mean.

Ascendant or Rising: The First of Four Important Critical Angles in a Horoscope

- How other people see you
- How you present yourself to the world
- Your physical appearance

First House: Personality

- Early childhood
- Your ego
- Your body type and how you feel about your body
- General physical health
- Defense mechanisms
- Your creative thrust

Second House: Personal Values

- How you earn and spend your money
- Your personal values
- Your material resources and assets
- Your attitudes and beliefs toward money
- Your possessions and your attitude toward those possessions
- Your self-worth
- Your attitudes about creativity

Third House: Communication and Learning

- Personal expression
- Intellect and mental attitudes and perceptions
- Siblings, neighbors, and relatives
- How you learn
- School until college
- Reading, writing, teaching
- Short trips (the grocery store versus Europe in seven days)
- Earth-bound transportation
- Creativity as a communication device

IC or Fourth House Cusp: The Second Critical Angle in a Horoscope

- Sign on IC describes the qualities and traits of your home during early childhood
- Describes roots of your creative abilities and talents

Fourth House: Your Roots

- Personal/domestic environment
- Your home
- Your attitudes toward family
- Early childhood conditioning
- Real estate
- Your nurturing parent

Some astrologers say this house belongs to Mom or her equivalent in your life, others say it belongs to Dad or his equivalent. It makes sense to us that it's Mom because the fourth house is ruled by the moon, which rules mothers. But in this day and age, when parental roles are in flux, the only hard and fast rule is that the fourth belongs to the parent who nurtures you most of the time.

- The conditions at the end of your life
- Early childhood support of your creativity and interests

Fifth House: Children and Creativity

- Kids, your firstborn in particular
- Love affairs, romance
- What you enjoy
- Creative ability
- Gambling and speculation
- Pets

Traditionally, pets belong in the sixth house. But that definition stems from the days when "pets" were chattel. These days we don't even refer to them as pets. They are animal companions who bring us pleasure.

Sixth House: Work and Responsibility

- Day-to-day working conditions and environment
- Competence and skills
- Your experience of employees and employers
- Duty to work, to employees
- Health and the daily maintenance of your health

Descendant/Seventh House Cusp: The Third Critical Angle in a Horoscope

- The sign on the house cusp describes the qualities sought in intimate or business relationships
- Describes qualities of creative partnerships

Seventh House: Partnerships and Marriage

- Marriage
- Marriage partner
- Significant others
- Business partnerships
- Close friends
- Open enemies
- Contracts

Eighth House: Transformation

- Sexuality as transformation
- Secrets

- Death, taxes, inheritances, insurance, mortgages and loans
- Resources shared with others
- Your partner's finances
- The occult (read: astrology, reincarnation, UFOs, everything weird and strange)
- Your hidden talents
- Psychology
- Life-threatening illnesses
- Your creative depths

Ninth House: Worldview

- Philosophy and religion
- The law, courts, judicial system
- Publishing
- Foreign travels and cultures
- College, graduate school
- Spiritual beliefs
- Travel abroad

MC or Cusp of Tenth House: The Fourth Critical Angle in a Horoscope

- Sign on cusp of MC describes qualities you seek in a profession
- Your public image
- Your creative and professional achievements

Tenth House: Profession and Career

- Public image as opposed to a job that merely pays the bills (sixth house)
- Your status and position in the world
- The authoritarian parent and authority in general
- People who hold power over you
- Your public life
- Your career/profession

Eleventh House: Ideals and Dreams

- Peer groups
- Social circles (your writers' group, your mother's bridge club)
- Your dreams and aspirations
- How you can realize your dreams

Twelfth House: Personal Unconscious

- Power you have disowned that must be claimed again
- Institutions—hospitals, prisons, nursing homes—and what is hidden
- What you must confront this time around, your karma, issues brought in from other lives
- Psychic gifts and abilities
- Healing talents
- What you give unconditionally

In the section on predictions you'll find references to transiting planets moving into certain houses. These houses are actually solar houses that are created by putting your sun sign on the ascendant. This technique is how most predictions are made for the general public rather than for specific individuals.

Lunations

Every year there are twelve new moons and twelve full moons, with some years having thirteen full moons. The extra full moon is called the Blue Moon. New moons are typically when we should begin new projects, set new goals, seek new opportunities. They're times for beginnings. They usher in new opportunities according to house and sign.

Two weeks after each new moon, there's a full moon. This is the time of harvest, fruition, when we reap what we've sown.

Whenever a new moon falls in your sign, take time to brainstorm what you would like to achieve during weeks and months until the full moon falls in your sign. These goals can be in any area of your life. Or you can simply take the time on each new moon to set up goals and strategies for what you would like to achieve or manifest during the next two weeks—until the full moon—or until the next new moon.

Here's a list of all the new moons and full moons during 2014. The asterisk beside any new-moon entry indicates a solar eclipse; the asterisk next to a full-moon entry indicates a lunar eclipse.

TABLE 3
LUNATIONS OF 2014

New Moons	Full Moons
January 1–Capricorn	January 15–Cancer
January 30–Aquarius	February 14–Leo
March 1–Pisces	March 16–Virgo
March 30–Aries	*April 15–Libra
April 29–Taurus*	May 14–Scorpio
May 28–Gemini	June 13–Sagittarius
June 27–Cancer	July 12–Capricorn
July 26–Leo	August 10–Aquarius
August 25–Virgo	September 8–Pisces
September 24–Libra	*October 8–Aries
October 23–Scorpio*	November 6–Taurus
November 22–Sagittarius	December 6–Gemini
December 21–Capricorn	

Every year there are two lunar and two solar eclipses, separated from one another by about two weeks. Lunar eclipses tend to deal with emotional issues, our internal world, and often bring an emotional issue to the surface related to the sign and house in which the eclipse falls. They can also result in news. Solar eclipses deal with events and often enable us to see something that has eluded us. They also symbolize beginnings and endings.

Read more about eclipses in the big picture for your sign for 2014. I also recommend Celeste Teal's excellent book, *Eclipses*.

Mercury Retrograde

Every year Mercury—the planet that symbolizes communication and travel—turns retrograde three times. During these periods our travel plans often go awry, communication breaks down, computers go berserk, cars or appliances develop problems. You get the idea. Things in our daily lives don't work as smoothly as we would like.

Here are some guidelines to follow for Mercury retrogrades:

Try not to travel. But if you have to, be flexible and think of it as an adventure. If you're stuck overnight in an airport in Houston or Atlanta, though, the adventure part of this could be a stretch.

Don't sign contracts—unless you don't mind revisiting them when Mercury is direct again.

Communicate as succinctly and clearly as possible.

Back up all computer files. Use an external hard drive and/or a flash drive. If you've had a computer crash, you already know how frustrating it can be to reconstruct your files.

Don't buy expensive electronics. Expensive anything.

Don't submit manuscripts, screenplays, pitch ideas, or launch new projects.

Revise, rewrite, rethink, review.

In the overview for each sign, check out the dates for this year's Mercury retrogrades and how these retrogrades are likely to impact you. Do the same for eclipses.

Other Retrogrades

Every planet except the sun and moon turns retrograde. So let's look at the retrogrades that will occur in 2014.

Venus: Retrograde in Capricorn from January 1 to January 31. This retro is continuation of one that began at the tail end of 2013. Venus retros can cause rough patches in your most intimate relationships. It can also bring about physical inconveniences and discomforts—your AC or heat goes out in the office, at home, or even in your car. Avoid buying luxury items during a Venus retro. That said, good deals can be found during a Venus retrograde. We once bought a car that we traded in a year later for the same price that we paid for it.

Mars: Retrograde in Libra from March 1 to May 19. Since Mars represents your sexuality, ambition, and physicality, best to check your natal chart to find out where you have Libra.

Jupiter: January 1 to March 6, retrograde in Cancer. This retro is a continuation from 2013. During this period your finances may be depressed, your luck factor isn't operating at full potential, and there could be setbacks or delays with publishing and educational ventures. Since the retro falls in Cancer, it's possible there are delays or setbacks at home too.

Saturn: March 2 to July 20. Retrograde in Scorpio. You discover which structures in your life need bolstering. Profits may be depressed.

Uranus: July 21 to December 21. Retrograde in Aries. Upheavals and changes occur, you feel unsettled, you may feel that your uniqueness is being squashed by a situation or relationship.

Neptune: June 9 to November 15. Retrograde in Pisces. Your creativity and ability to envision what you desire are limited in some way.

Pluto: April 14 to September 22. Retrograde in Capricorn. You may feel powerless or unmotivated in some area of your life.

CHAPTER 3

Love and Romance in 2014

Regardless of what kind of craziness is going on in the world around us, we still fall in love, commit to someone, get engaged or married. But our lives are certainly influenced by our environments, and in changing times we may become more independent or needier, our priorities may shift, or we may reach out for new relationships because we have outgrown the old ones. Or they may have outgrown us.

Let's start with your natal Venus. If you don't know what sign and house Venus was in when you were born, check http://www.astro.com/cgi/ade.cgi and enter your birth data. If you don't know the exact time of your birth, put in twelve noon so you can at least see what sign Venus was in when you were born.

The sign and house placement of your natal Venus tells you a great deal about your capacity for loving another and for being loved and your attitudes about love and romance. It also reveals how you approach your creativity, money, beauty, and females. If you're a Taurus or a Libra, Venus rules your sign, and if you have either of those signs rising, Venus rules your chart. It means the placement of Venus in your natal chart is particularly important.

In a man's chart the sign and house placement of Venus can indicate the kind of women to whom he's attracted. It can also reveal something about his relationship with his daughter, if he has one. In a woman's chart Venus indicates relationships with other women and with a daughter, if she has one.

So let's take a look at what your natal Venus means in terms of its sign and house placement:

Venus in the Signs

Venus in Aries

You take risks in romantic relationships. You tend to be passionate and impulsive and may be somewhat self-centered when it comes to romance and love. You're a terrific initiator when it comes to making money, but your money may go out as fast as it comes in. You're also adept at initiating creative projects, but if you lose interest along the way, you drop the project and move on to something new.

Venus in Taurus

Venus rules Taurus, so it's happy here and functions well. You're a sensuous individual, at times even lusty. You form deep emotional attachments in love and romance, and once you meet the right person are fully committed. You can be exceptionally stubborn about having things your way in a relationship. You attract money and prosperity, particularly if you work actively with your beliefs. Your creative expression is heightened by your sensuality. Once you start something, you're rarely a quitter!

Venus in Gemini

You have great charm and wit and can talk to anyone about anything. Your romantic relationships may not last long, and you may be involved with several people at once. You're not consciously fickle, but you simply get bored easily and move on. Two marriages are possible. On the creative front, you have so many interests and talents that it's sometimes difficult for you to choose what you would like to do most. Self-expression comes easily to you.

Venus in Cancer

You're a nurturing, compassionate individual. Home and marriage are important to you, and your family ties are strong. When you commit to a relationship, you commit completely. But until you're committed, there can be a tendency toward secret love affairs. You nurture your own creative abilities and skills with a resoluteness that others admire. You're not a quitter any more than Venus in Taurus is! You benefit through real estate and land and spend money freely on your home and family.

Venus in Leo

Like Venus in Aries, you have great passion and are ardent in your relationships. Your gregarious nature makes you the life of any party and attracts romantic interests easily and with hardly any effort on your part. In any romantic relationship, though, you like your partner to compliment you, notice you, court, and seduce you. You may have creative talent in the performing arts—theater, dance—or become publicly prominent.

Venus in Virgo

You have discriminating tastes in romantic relationships and may keep a mental list of qualities a partner must have. You're analytical about love—until the right person enters your life and sweeps you away. Then that mental list goes straight out the window. You can be self-critical in a relationship and also critical of your partner or about elements in the relationship. The quest of Venus in Virgo is to polish the diamond until it's the best there is. When it comes to artistic expression, you're a perfectionist, the kind of person who insists that all Ts are crossed. You're exceptionally good at any form of communication.

Venus in Libra

Venus rules this sign, so the planet is happy here, just as it is in Taurus. In romance and love you may have an idealized picture of how things are supposed to be and may bend over backward to make that idealized version happen. You seek harmony and peace in all your relationships—the very things that may elude you. Your artistic strengths are considerable and varied. There may be talent with writing, music, art, photography, or singing. You enjoy beauty in all its forms and don't hesitate to spend money on the things you love.

Venus in Scorpio

You have a passionate, sexual nature and are forever seeking the absolute bottom line in a relationship. When someone interests you, that person's pubic persona isn't enough for you. You dig deeper, scratching way beneath the surface, uncovering the individual's secrets and his or her hidden life. This propensity can lead to stormy relationships until you meet someone who erects strong boundaries. Your creativity springs from the deepest levels of your being and is often inspired. You might, for instance, be a pianist who can't read music and plays entirely by ear. Or you might be an artist who never took an art lesson in your life.

Venus in Sagittarius

Just like Venus in Aries and Leo, the other two fire signs, you love passionately. Your generous nature sometimes prompts you to wear your heart on your sleeve. You seek a partner who loves to travel as much as you do and who shares your love of animals and the arts. But when your personal freedom is threatened in some way, when a relationship makes you feel penned in, your passion cools quickly, and you immediately extricate yourself from the relationship. Creatively you seek the larger picture of whatever you're doing and leave the finer details to others.

Venus in Capricorn

Your capacity for love runs deep, but you are often restrained in how you express it. This restraint may be the result of a lack of trust in yourself or the other person, but it can also simply be one of your patterns, something that began when you were very young. Sexually however all the restraints and reserve fall away and your true passions burst forth. You strive to achieve financial and material assets and work hard to do so.

Venus in Aquarius

For you love and romance must start with an intellectual camaraderie, an exchange of ideas. You enjoy the company of idiosyncratic individuals, people out of the mainstream who have unusual ideas, occupations, or perceptions. You have many friends and among them may be a person who interests you romantically. In romantic relationships you need intellectual stimulation. Your financial habits could be erratic, or you may earn your living in an unusual way. Creatively you're a trendsetter.

Venus in Pisces

Your compassionate nature is practically legendary among people who know you. In love you're a true romantic, the kind of person who enjoys moonlit walks on beaches. It's this idealism, though, that sometimes gets you into trouble if the reality doesn't measure up. In a relationship your sensitivity to your partner's moods often borders on psychic. Romantic relationships and emotional attachments are necessary for your well-being.

Venus in the Houses

First house

You're a natural charmer, friendly, and probably physically attractive. You may have some unique talent that finds expression in art or music. You love literature and poetry and have a fondness for beautiful surroundings. This placement is usually fortunate—unless Venus is poorly aspected—and things generally come to you with ease. The closer Venus is to the ascendant—the rising—the more pronounced these qualities are.

Second house

Financial comfort, perhaps even wealth. You benefit financially from marriage and partnerships. You're probably an extravagant spender, but you can usually afford it, so it's not an issue. Your personal values are important to you, and you spend time and effort developing them.

Third house

You converse easily with people and are comfortable in your neighborhood or community. You're close to your siblings, other relatives, and neighbors and have excellent rapport with your immediate family. The love of your life may be someone you meet in your community or through relatives.

Fourth house

Your home and family are important to you and vital to your well-being. You seek harmony in your domestic environment and go to great lengths to maintain it. It's possible that you meet the love of your life early in life and then meet again later on when you're adults. You have a great rapport with your parents and gain financially through them. The closer Venus is to the cusp of the fourth house, the more pronounced these attributes will be.

Fifth house

For love, romance, children, and creative endeavors, this is where Venus is really at home. The fifth-house placement is great for happy love affairs, artistic projects, and anything creative. Your children may have unusual talents. You gain through romantic partners, children, and any sort of creative endeavor. Your undoing may be excessive pleasure!

Sixth house

Your daily work is a source of pleasure for you. You enjoy what you do, whatever it is, and probably have harmonious relationships with your coworkers. You're able to integrate your creativity into your daily work, and other people appreciate and admire your work.

This placement favors good health generally, but you should avoid excessive use of alcohol and drugs. In terms of romance you may work with the one you love!

Seventh house

Venus is happy here. It's likely that you'll have a happy marriage and profitable partnerships generally. You and your partner may work together in some capacity, perhaps moving toward a common goal— self-employment, for instance. You're a magnet for attracting what you need in partnerships and financial benefits.

Eighth house

You gain financially through marriage and partnerships, inheritances, taxes, and contracts. You're lucky when it comes to other people's money and resources. You may have unusual and positive experiences with metaphysics. Love and romance with someone you knew in a past life are possible.

Ninth house

Romance and love may find you while you're traveling overseas. Music and art with spiritual themes intrigue you, and you may have talent yourself in these areas. This placement of Venus favors involvement with publishing, spiritual groups, higher education, and foreign travel.

Tenth house

Talk about popularity! Writers, artists, entertainers, actors, novelists, reporters, and diplomats are all indicated by this placement. You're at ease in any kind of social venue, and other people are attracted to you and your ideas. Career matters and your professional life generally tend to unfold smoothly with little effort on your part. You may be "married" to your career or find love with someone who works in your profession. The closer Venus falls to the cusp of the tenth house, the more pronounced the qualities.

Eleventh house

Friendships and groups are important to you. They help you to achieve your wishes and dreams and share your interests in the arts, music, and books. You invest a lot of time and energy in your friendships, particularly with women, and could meet someone special through friends.

Twelfth house

Secret love affairs and romantic intrigues are indicated. You may work in solitude or behind the scenes in some sort of artistic profession. You enjoy mystery and adventure and actually enjoy the dramas of romantic intrigues.

Venus Transits and Retrogrades

Unless Venus is retrograde, as it is in 2014, a Venus transit lasts from three to four weeks. The times to watch for are when Venus returns to the place where it was when you were born and when Venus conjuncts your sun.

The first period is called a Venus return and is usually a genuinely enjoyable period. You have all the support you need or want from friends and partners. Everything that is promised in the natal placement of Venus is enhanced.

The second period is also terrific. It enhances all the qualities of your sun sign, bolsters your self-confidence, artistic inspirations, and ambitions and should do wonders for your love life.

In 2014 Venus begins the year retrograde in Capricorn and turns direct on January 31. These retrograde periods can be tough on your love life and your artistic expression. Or you may find yourself dealing with issues from the past in either of these areas. Another possibility with Venus retrograde is that your physical comfort may be compromised in some way. Perhaps the air conditioning or heat in your office building goes on the fritz, or maybe the defroster, heat, or AC in your car stops working.

This year, Venus transits Capricorn twice—at the beginning of the year and again briefly at the end. In between it moves through all the other signs as well. For specifics on how Venus transits affect your sign, read chapter 14.

CHAPTER 4

Finances in 2014

More than four years after the financial meltdown in 2008—when the "too big to fail" banks were bailed out, the housing market bottomed out, and unemployment burgeoned—the situation hasn't improved.

According to www.forecasts.org, unemployment by the spring of 2012 is supposed to be at 10.3 percent, and unless the economy turns around, that figure may be much higher by 2014. Despite the Obama administration's "homeowner bailout" programs, six million Americans are either behind on their mortgage payments or facing foreclosure, and millions more are underwater on their mortgages. An article in the *Las Vegas Sun* estimates that as of late 2011 American homeowners owe $700 billion to $800 billion more than their homes are actually worth.

A report in Huffington Post in October 2011 revealed half of borrowers with prime loans—those loans made to individuals with good credit and income—will likely end up underwater. A Fitch ratings report found that with home prices expected to drop in value by another 10 percent, at least half of prime borrowers will end up underwater. Complicating the situation, of course, are unemployment, underemployment, and the rising costs of goods.

How fast are those costs rising? Do your own test. What products do you use regularly? How much have their prices risen in the past year? A year ago our favorite coffee, a Cuban brand, used to sell for $2.59 a pound. The price has doubled. A dozen eggs that cost a buck a year ago are now twice that. A loaf of bread that used to cost a buck now costs three times that. You get the idea here, and you've no doubt noticed the rise in costs in your own life just for basics. When you include the prices of gasoline, electricity, tuition for college, and everything else, it's no wonder the middle class is shrinking.

The reality points to a pattern that has been prevalent throughout the twenty-first century—greed. Whether it's corporate or individual greed, there are no free rides. Banks lent to people who didn't have the income to meet mortgage payments and bundled good and bad mortgages together and sold them off. Borrowers used their homes as ATM machines. In a sense what is happening to the American economy is a reflection of what has happened to the U.S. economy overall: we are living beyond our means.

On the other hand, there are plenty of homeowners who weren't living beyond their means but whose lives changed dramatically when they were laid off or got sick, or their income was somehow diminished. You probably know people in your own community who have suffered in this way.

So what do all these depressing statistics means for you in 2014? A couple of things. If you've been hit badly by this economy, the first thing you should so is become politically active. It's not enough to vote in elections. Democracy is also about expressing your opinion. Occupy Wall Street started as a genuine grassroots movement and hit a nerve with the nation's young people. What started as a small protest on September 17, 2011, became a global movement within a month. That kind of activism is what helps to usher in a change in the status quo.

Take stock of your particular abilities and talents. Is there something you can do that would fill a niche in the market? Adversity, after all, can be an opportunity that prompts you to perceive your own skills in a different way and to see the market with new eyes.

What can you change about the way you live? Do you stash away a percentage of everything you make? Do you spend money as quickly as it comes in? Do you have a realistic budget? Are you in credit card debt? Do you live debt free? Depending on your financial situation, here are tips for each sign on how to maximize your potential this year; when the stars favor your finances—and when they don't.

But first take this inventory about your beliefs concerning money.

Belief Inventory

Here's a list of some commonly held negative beliefs about money. Check the ones to which you subscribe:

- Money is the root of all evil
- Money is nonspiritual

- The rich have major problems in their lives
- Money corrupts
- If you have too much money, you have to worry about losing it
- If you have too much money, it takes over your life.
- The wealthy don't have money problems, but they have a lot of other problems.

Many of these beliefs we've adopted from family and peers and have held on to them because they're comfortable, we believe they're true, or because we don't even realize we believe them! So if you're not satisfied with what you're earning, start monitoring how you think about money. Any time you find yourself thinking a negative thought about money, turn the thought around by thinking something more positive. Also, read Napoleon Hills' classic *Think and Grow Rich* and *Money and the Law of Attraction* by Esther and Jerry Hicks.

Now let's take a look at how you can maximize your earning potential in 2014.

Aries

There's a reason you're called the trailblazer, the entrepreneur. You see opportunities where others may not and figure out a way to turn those opportunities into money. You're the type who, in the midst of the Great Depression, might have launched your own business and filled a gap you recognized in the market. Adversity doesn't scare you; it becomes your booster rocket.

There are two excellent periods this year for finances. The first period falls between May 2 and 28, when Venus is in your sign. This period is excellent for earning additional money, sales, and asking for a raise. The second period, when Venus transits Taurus and your financial area, falls between May 28 and June 23. During this period you may be more prone toward saving rather than spending. But if you do feel the urge to spend, it may be for high-end items—art, jewelry. So if you succumb to the urge, be sure to pay cash!

Although we talk about Jupiter transits in a later chapter, this planet's transit through fellow fire sign Leo could be quite nice for your finances. That time frame: July 16, 2014, to August 11, 2015.

Excellent backup dates: September 13 to October 26, when Mars transits fellow fire sign Sagittarius.

Taurus

Many of you are artistic, good with money and investments, fashion, the culinary arts, photography, writing, music. In fact, you probably have numerous talents but because you tend to be somewhat reserved, other people don't know about them. Well, now is the time to let your true self shine, Taurus. And once you do, once you embrace all you are, then the opportunities begin to arrive, and you may have a chance to earn your living doing what you love.

An excellent time this year for maximizing your earning potential falls between May 28 and June 23, when Venus is in your sign. This period is one in which you feel extremely good about yourself and life in general, and that feeling bolsters your self-confidence. Others pick up on this, and suddenly, Taurus, you can do no wrong. You get hired for that job you want; you land a promotion or raise; you sell your novel.

The next period that could pay off financially falls between January 1 and July 16, when Jupiter transits Cancer, a water sign compatible with your earth-sign sun. This occurs in your solar third house of communication and travel. No telling what treasures you may discover during this transit. Perhaps your Web site wins an award. Or you sell your novel. Or you become a travel writer.

Good backup dates: October 26 to December 4, when Mars transits fellow earth sign Capricorn, your solar ninth house. Your ambitions lead you in new directions—perhaps overseas, into publishing, or higher education. Maybe law school is in your future!

Gemini

Left to your own devices, things like checkbooks and saving accounts and IRAs and investments are for other people to ponder, such as your accountant, partner, parents, or sibling. You would rather write and talk about *ideas*. So let's talk about the *idea* of money. What does it actually represent to you? Energy? Freedom? Albatross? During 2014 it's to your advantage to look at money as energy and freedom. The more you make, the greater your freedom to do what interests you. The more effort you expend, the greater the energy you're putting into what you do and the greater the return. At least that's how it's supposed to work in theory. But you have to remain focused and resolute.

Most Geminis are versatile and adaptable, and many are excellent communicators. How can you use those particular skills and talents to earn an income?

One of your best times this year for increasing your earnings falls between January 1 and July 16, when Jupiter transits Cancer, your solar second house of finances. This transit has been going on since 2013, so by now you should have a clear idea how it works and the kind of luck and expansion that accompanies it.

Another excellent period for increasing your earnings occurs between June 23 and July 18, when Venus transits your sign. Things may seem to be going so well that you could be tempted to kick back and chill. Resist that temptation! Use this time frame to move forward—ask for a raise, apply for a promotion, or look for a new job that pays more.

An excellent backup period is September 13 to October 26, when Mars transits fire sign Sagittarius, your solar seventh house. This transit could bring exactly the right business partner you need. Or you and your spouse or partner go into business together.

Cancer

Your imagination and intuition should serve you well this year, particularly if you use both to expand your income. You tend to be good at budgeting your money and usually know what you earn, spend, and on what. Even though you probably aren't obsessed about money, you find a sense of security in having money in savings that you can draw on when you need to.

This year there are several periods that favor your finances. The first occurs between July 18 and August

12, when Venus transits your sign. During this period ask for a raise or promotion, apply for new jobs, network with professional peers, or open an IRA. Lucky you, this transit occurs just after the Mercury retrograde in your sign ends. Those dates: June 7 to July 1. Reread the section on Mercury retrogrades in chapter 2.

The second period when your finances—and just about everything else in your life—may undergo radical expansion occurs between January 1 and July 16, while expansive Jupiter transits your sign. This transit has been going on since last June, so you undoubtedly have a good idea already about the kinds of events and opportunities that Jupiter often brings.

Excellent backup dates: August 12 to September 5, when Venus transits Leo and your financial area. This period could bring a new source of income.

Leo

In 2014 the secret to staying afloat financially is twofold. First, have the facts at your fingertips. Know how much you actually bring home after taxes and FICA and any other fees that are automatically deducted from your income. Can you live on your take-home pay? If not, where can you cut back in your budget? Do you and your partner eat out frequently? Is it necessary? Do you go on shopping sprees? Keep track of your expenses for a couple of weeks for a more accurate picture of what comes in—and goes out.

Second, as one of the most flamboyant and theatrical signs of the zodiac, you probably like to look your best when in public. Be sure to budget for that—

clothing, shoes, hairstylists, spas—whatever it takes to maintain your public persona. But instead of shopping at the upscale shops, perhaps you can do equally well in thrift stores.

There are some excellent periods in 2014 for increasing your earnings. The first period falls between August 12 and September 5, when Venus transits your sign. This one boosts self-confidence, other people find you infinitely appealing, and you can do no wrong, Leo. So ask for a raise or promotion or send out résumés. Unexpected bonuses or royalties could arrive during this time. If so, stash the money in an IRA.

The next period falls between July 16, 2014, and August 11, 2015, when Jupiter transits your sign. Expansive Jupiter seeks to improve your life in all areas during this transit.

Excellent backup dates: September 5 to 29, when Venus moves through Virgo, your financial area. This period favors details and enables you to connect all the dots.

Virgo

You're the most discriminating of signs—measured, diligent, with a penchant for details. You can be something of a perfectionist too, but rarely demand of others what you demand of yourself. Whatever you take on, you do so with complete dedication. So in 2014 perfect your finances, Virgo. Set your monetary goals and then figure out how best to achieve them.

One of the most favorable periods for earning more falls between September 5 and 29, when Venus transits your sign. This period is favorable for landing a raise or promotion, for receiving money from unexpected sources—an insurance payment, a royalty check—and for sending out résumés for a job that pays you more. It's also good for pitching manuscripts and screenplays.

Another potentially profitable period occurs between January 1 and July 16, when expansive Jupiter transits compatible water sign Cancer and forms a beneficial angle to your sun. Friends and any groups to which you belong prove helpful. This period is when you're in the right place at the right time to bolster your bank account, land a raise, or make money by expanding your services or products to overseas markets.

Excellent backup dates: September 29 to October 23, when Venus transits Libra, your financial area.

Libra

Your sign, like Taurus, is Venus ruled, so its transits are particularly important to you. You feel more comfortable and balanced when surrounded by beauty—fresh flowers, art, pleasing furniture, perhaps even some sort of unique collection that has good memories attached to it. Music and books may be important to you too, and perhaps some of your disposable income goes toward these things.

Between September 29 and October 23 Venus transits your sign. This period should be particularly good for you. Venus is happy in your sign and can help you to bring in additional income from a variety of different sources. If you're in sales, you can sell anything to anyone. You might sell a manuscript, piece of art, or some other product born of your creativity.

During Jupiter's transit of compatible fire sign Leo, between July 16, 2014, and August 11, 2015, you may experience an expansion in your income that seems to happen without any effort on your part. That's an illusion, of course. You have been seeding the possibilities for quite a while now. Jupiter means expansion, and its energy can be used wherever you apply your attention and energy.

Excellent backup dates: March 1 to May 19, when Mars is in direct motion in your sign. This one acts like a booster rocket!

Scorpio

As a fixed water sign and the most emotionally intense sign in the zodiac, you're no stranger to transformation. With Pluto as the ruler of your sign, your life is constantly undergoing transformation of some kind. But if you would like to bolster and transform your finances, 2014 is a great year to do it. Your considerable intuition and ability to get to the absolute bottom line of anything you research and investigate serve you well this year.

Between October 23 and November 16 Venus transits your sign. So during this period ask for a raise, apply for a promotion, or send out résumés for jobs that really interest you. Be proactive. You and your ideas appeal to others. Your charisma intrigues them, so use it to your advantage.

Another excellent period for expanding your income occurs between January 1 and July 16, 2014, when Jupiter transits fellow water sign Cancer and forms a beneficial angle to your sun. This period should be productive for you, with new creative opportunities that could bring in additional income.

Saturn begins the year in your sign, Scorpio, which should bring stability and structure to your finances and other areas of your life. It's retrograde between March 2 and July 20, so it essentially enters a dormant state during this period. But before the retrograde and afterward, until it enters Sagittarius on December 23, use its energy to build a more solid financial foundation for yourself.

Excellent backup dates: July 25 to September 13, when Mars, your coruler, transits your sign. This one is your booster rocket and confers enormous physical energy and resolve.

Sagittarius

Let the good times roll . . . and roll! As a mutable fire sign, your life is about activity and forward motion. You don't have time for things like budgets, balancing a checkbook, and keeping track of what you earn and spend. Then when it's time to do your taxes, you freak out. You can't find receipts, your files are messed up . . . you get the idea.

In 2013 we advised you to organize your finances. If you did that, in 2014 your finances should be much easier to navigate. You'll be alert for the periods when it will be easier to increase your income. More money means more travel, and any Sadge loves that idea!

Between November 16 and December 10 Venus transits your sign. Not only does your self-confidence soar, but others find you appealing and want you on their team. So ask for a raise or promotion, pitch your ideas, or submit your manuscript or screenplay or some other product you have created.

Between January 31 and March 5 and December 10, 2014, and January 4, 2015, Venus in direct motion transits Capricorn, your financial area. These two periods should prompt you to be careful with your money, particularly as your income increases. Just because you have more money in your pocket, Sadge, doesn't mean it should go out as quickly as it comes in. Capricorn is a grounded, focused sign, and as Venus moves through it you learn the wisdom of saving.

Another excellent period for you and your money should occur during Jupiter's thirteen-month transit through fellow fire sign Leo. This one should increase not only your finances but also opportunities in whatever area you place your attention.

Capricorn

As a cardinal earth sign, you build your financial world just as you do everything else, one brick at a time. You do it patiently, methodically, and usually have a goal in mind—double your earnings in six months, for instance. Or pay off your mortgage in the next two years.

In 2014 you have several windows of opportunity when it's easier to increase your earnings, launch a business, pitch an idea that someone will buy, or sell a book. Luck is on your side; you're in the right place at the right time; you meet exactly the right people who make things happen. The first period falls between January 31 and March 5; the second period is between December 10, 2014, and January 4, 2015, when Venus is moving direct through your sign. This transit is a confidence booster. When you feel good about yourself, others pick up on it, and suddenly everything flows your way. If you're looking for a better-paying job or a second job, then this period could bring news.

The second period occurs between January 1 and July 16 when Jupiter transits your opposite sign, Cancer. This transit should expand your professional partnerships, which in turn could be very positive for your finances.

You have an additional plus this year. Saturn is in Scorpio until December 23, forming a strong and beneficial angle to your sun. This transit helps you to build solid financial foundations.

Aquarius

You don't really fit into any financial category. Some Aquarians are great with money; others aren't. Some are savers; others are spenders. But one thing is for sure. When you make up your mind to do something, you do it. No one and nothing can sway you from a path you've chosen. So for 2014 let's look at times when your income can increase.

One of the most favorable periods falls between March 5 and April 5. Venus transits your sign, suggesting that your appeal is broad and others like you and your ideas, making this an ideal time to ask for a raise. Ask with the expectation that the raise will be given. Whether you're sending out résumés or interviewing for jobs, you're in your element and should reap the rewards you so justly deserve.

Another good period falls between April 5 and

May 2, when Venus moves through Pisces, your financial area. You may have a tough time making up your mind if you're given choices about your money. But once you do make up your mind, this transit could bring about a raise, result in the repayment of a loan, or perhaps bring in an insurance payment or tax break.

Excellent backup dates: December 4, 2014, to January 12, 2015. Mars is in your sign, and it's your booster rocket, Aquarius.

Pisces

Your considerable imagination and intuition will prove enormously valuable in this year of transformation. Whatever you can imagine, after all, can manifest itself. So if you're imagining a quantum leap in your income, Pisces, fix a figure firmly in mind, focus on it, release it—and let the universe figure out the connections that must be made for you to earn that amount of money.

In the interim, of course, it's smart not to just sit back but to become more proactive. If you dislike your job, figure out what you would like to be doing and start submitting applications and résumés. If you often find yourself short of money, set up a realistic budget and try to stick to it. You know, do the small stuff!

Timing is essential, so let's take a look at the windows of opportunity in 2014 when things really flow your way. These periods are when you should ask for a raise or promotion, submit résumés, schedule interviews, do whatever you can to earn more. The first period falls between April 5 and May 2, when Venus transits your sign. This is when you're more you than ever! Turn on the charm, let your muse in 24/7.

The second period falls between January 1 and July 16, when expansive Jupiter transits fellow water sign Cancer and forms a beneficial angle to your sun. Expansion, luck, you're in the right place at the right time!

CHAPTER 5

Lunar Madness in 2014

Collective Concepts of the Moon

There is something truly magical about the moon. As the closest celestial body to Earth, it has captured man's imagination for millennia. It has been the stuff of myths and fairy tales, poetry and legends. It has been worshipped and cursed and endowed with magical and curative powers. Religions have grown up around it. Sacrifices have been made to it.

In ancient cultures the passage of time was marked according to the lunation—or cycle—of the moon. A *month* was the time between one new moon and the next, and in a typical year there were thirteen lunar cycles. This way of marking time still exists among some pagan sects and may be closer to our natural rhythms than our present solar calendar.

Early shamans may have timed certain rituals according to the phases of the moon. Tribal people often planted crops during a new moon and harvested at a full moon. In the eighth century B.C. various civilizations discarded their 360-day calendar and based the calendar on observations of the sky. In ancient Rome priests observed the heavens and were supposed to announce to the emperor when a new month began. The month usually began with a new moon. This practice was also used by the Celts and Babylonians.

In the early fifties the moon was a favorite theme in science fiction books and movies, and the storylines rarely varied: the aliens came from the moon, we colonized the moon, or the moon fell out of orbit . . . you get the general picture. Even Disney issued movies in which the moon played a vital role. In one film, a Western, a woman who wore a hoop skirt typical of the American west started bouncing and kept bouncing higher and higher until she bounced right into the moon. The shadow you see in the moon is, according to Disney, that woman in the hoop skirt.

In 1969 Neil Armstrong took one giant leap for mankind, and our concept of the moon was forever changed. Even though its relative position in the sky hadn't changed, everything else about it had.

We now had some idea what it really looked like, and the news was far from good. Dust, dust, and more dust. A black vacuum. Unimaginable cold. Nothingness. What's most vivid in our minds, though, is how the Earth looked from the moon—a swirling turquoise gem 240,000 miles distant, a blue pearl turning in space. Our planet literally looked alive.

This was the year when Vietnam was in full swing. Americans arrived home in body bags, riots swept across college campuses, LSD was the drug of choice. People were tuning in and dropping out faster than the pictures of the moon were beamed back to earth.

This was the year that half a million people converged on the tiny town of Woodstock, New York, to hear Hendrix, Baez, Dylan, Joplin, and all the other musicians who had captured the emotional reality of war and chaos. Women threw off their shackles. Carlos Castaneda and Aldous Huxley hurled open the doors to other realities. Camelot was dead, Martin Luther King was dead, and we had walked on the moon.

In many ways those steps of Armstrong's signaled that we were ready to confront our unconscious selves, our feminine, intuitive selves.

Fast-forward to the summer of 1997, July 4 to be exact. In the opening scenes of the movie *Independence Day* a mammoth shadow falls across the surface of the moon. A moving shadow whose shape is unmistakable. The message comes through loud and clear: the shadow is that of a spaceship that uses the moon as a base, and now that ship is on the move toward Earth. What ensues is pure Hollywood, with Will Smith holding the record for aliens annihilated. But *Independence Day*, like Armstrong's one giant leap, is part of our contemporary, collective perceptions of the moon, its essential beauty and sublime mysteries.

Despite Hollywood and NASA, each of us has some personal concept about the moon. After all, we drop our heads back on any given night, and there it is, shaped like a ubiquitous eye or the grin of a Cheshire cat or like a piece of fruit with the top lopped off. It speaks to us. We speak to it. Romance, madness, werewolves, witches, pagans, Druids, ocean tides and blood tides, or a sharp rise in murder and mayhem: it's all fair game where the moon is concerned. Every notion that we hold about the moon is true *for us,* and that subjective texture is certainly in keeping with the nature of the moon in astrology.

If the sun is where you shine in your corner of the universe, the moon is your personal oracle. If the sun represents your life force, the moon represents the internal landscape that supports and maintains the life force. In astrology lunar energy is embodied in that mythological moment when Luke Skywalker recognizes that Darth Vader is his father or when, in *ET,* the alien is getting drunk and the boy is trying to dissect a frog at school and their psyches mesh. Lunar energy is operating when reality splits off for the character Gwyneth Paltrow plays in *Sliding Doors* or during the love scene in *Titanic.*

Lunar energy is the MO in *Thelma and Louise, Jacob's Ladder,* and *What Dreams May Come.* It's the psychic visions the young boy has in *The Shining* or the visions another young boy has in *The Sixth Sense.* It's the mother's anguish in *The Deep End of the Ocean.* Without lunar energy we would be empty shells, automatons, the burn-the-books society in *Fahrenheit 451.* We would be Keanu Reeves still stuck in the matrix, powerless puppets who accept everything at face value.

Lunar Facts and Oddities

Most of us learn facts about the moon in grade-school science class. Today's kids have a distinct advantage over their parents of course because we've already been to the moon, and information is so readily accessible through the Internet.

The moon is our only satellite, and its average distance from Earth is 238,857 miles. Its revolution around the Earth takes twenty-seven days, seven hours, and forty-three minutes. Even though it's only a quarter the size of Earth, its gravitational pull is the main cause of our ocean tides. In fact, the moon actually has more than twice the effect on tides than the sun.

Since our bodies are primarily water, the moon's gravitational pull on the tides also affects our bodily fluids, metabolic rates, and of course our emotions. The link, for instance, between the full moon and violent aggression has been noted for years by police officers, hospital workers, and employees at mental institutions.

In the 1970s a Miami psychiatrist, Arnold Lieber, decided to conduct a scientific study to find out if these observations were true. As a med student at Jackson Memorial Hospital in Miami he'd noticed recurring periods when patients on the psyche ward were more disturbed than usual. These periods would last for several days, then the patients would resume their normal behavior. He became curious about the phenomenon and finally conducted a scientific study. His findings, later backed by four other independent studies, confirmed that during the full moon and, to a lesser extent, the new moon, there are increases in all violent crimes—homicide, rape, assault. There's also an increase in lesser crimes—burglary, auto theft, larceny, and drunken and disorderly behavior.

Is it any coincidence, then, that the word *lunatic* is derived from the word *lunar*?

Hospital workers and maternity ward nurses have

long noticed that more babies are born at the full and new moons than at any other time of the month. These may be due to the fact that the gravitational pull is strongest when the moon, sun, and Earth are aligned, as they are during the new and full moons. These observations have been backed by scientific studies. Interestingly enough, the lunar calendar is still the basis for calculating a pregnancy. The nine months are synodic months (the length of time it takes the moon to orbit Earth).

Since the moon has no atmosphere, it has nothing to protect it from meteor strikes, which is why its surface is pocked with impact craters. Since it has no tectonic or volcanic activity, its surface is immune to the erosive effects of atmospheric weathering, tectonic shifts, and volcanic upheavals that reshape the surface of our planet. In comparison, Earth is a work in progress. On the moon, even the footprints left by the Apollo astronauts will remain intact for millions of years unless a meteor strike obliterates them.

The moon's gravity is about a sixth of ours; that's why the Apollo astronauts looked like they were jumping rope up there. Despite appearances to the contrary, the moon has no light of its own. That gorgeous full moon you see each month is the reflected light of our sun.

Astrological Lunar Facts

The moon in your horoscope is every bit as important as your sun sign. In fact, Eastern astrologers give the moon greater emphasis than the sun sign. The moon rules the sign of Cancer and the fourth house in the horoscope. It represents mom or whoever plays that role for you and also symbolizes other women in your life. The moon is feminine, yin, our intuitive selves.

In the physical body her territory pertains primarily to women—breasts, ovaries, womb. In both genders she rules internal fluids and the stomach, and of course she's our emotional barometer, the gauge of our inner health. Not surprisingly, the moon rules conception.

A Czech physician, in fact, theorized that every woman had a fertility cycle that depended on the phase of the moon when she was born. Eugene Jones developed a fertilization calendar based on his theory, which allegedly showed a 98 percent success rate. He charged an astronomical fee for his calendar, but people who were desperate for children paid it.

Jones claimed that if a woman used his methods, she could choose the gender of her child. His technique was based on the rules of classical astrology, which he'd studied, and boils down to using the gender of moon signs. If conception took place on a Leo day, the child would be male. On a Taurus day, the child would be a girl.

The medical establishment went berserk over his claims. But when a panel of gynecologists challenged him to predict the genders of babies based only on their conception dates, Jones' accuracy was 87 percent.

If you don't know the sign of your natal moon, check on any of the astrology sites listed in this book and get a free birth chart. You'll need your exact time of birth, place, and of course the date!

The Transiting Moon

The moon changes signs every two and a half days. As you follow along in the daily prediction section for your sign, you'll be able to keep tabs on where the moon is on any given day. In the daily predictions we note when the moon is new or full. New moons favor new beginnings. Quite often around the time of the new moon you may receive good news about a project, relationship, or a financial or family matter. Full moons often coincide with completions, culminations, and news that ties up loose ends.

Certain activities are favored on certain lunar days, so let's take a look at how you can maximize the transiting moon's energy in your life.

Aries Moon

Cardinal Fire Sign

This is the day to be a fearless entrepreneur, to move forward on projects that have been sitting on the back burner for weeks or months. It's a great time to initiate new projects too, especially those that have been rattling around in the back of your head for some time.

You may feel restless and impatient with others, so the best way to deal with it is to pour that energy into something about which you feel passionate. Others see you as a leader, as the person with answers. You attract individuals who are eager to be on your team. You feel more self-sufficient, capable of doing whatever needs to be done.

Follow your impulses regardless of how odd they may seem. Sometimes our impulses are the universe's way of leading us toward a new opportunity, relationship, or creative project. Since Mars rules Aries, physical activity is heightened. Take a yoga class. Join the gym. Go walking. Weather permitting, it's a great day for a hike, bike ride, or long swim.

It's a good day to *believe* that whatever you desire can manifest itself. Your intentions and focus are key.

Taurus Moon

Fixed Earth Sign

The moon loves Taurus as much as it loves Cancer, the sign that it rules. In Taurus lunar energies work effortlessly and smoothly, and that makes your intuition easier to develop and use.

On a Taurus moon day think about that children's story *Ferdinand the Bull*. The author probably wasn't thinking about Taurus when he created the character, but Ferdinand is the perfect archetype for Taurus. Ferdinand enjoyed peaceful surroundings, and today so do you. In fact, peacefulness and harmony are vital to your emotional well-being. You need these qualities the way a Gemini moon needs books or education or communication with other people.

It will take a lot to anger you today, but repeated provocation can trigger your "bull's rush" fury, the human equivalent of Ferdinand's reaction to the bee sting. Some of the things that can set you off are incessant nagging by someone who wants you to do something you don't want to do, insistence that you act in a particular way, unreasonable demands or actions by anyone.

A Taurus moon day enables you to stick with something right to the end. You won't be a quitter. You will also be slow to change your mind and opinion and won't be rushed or cajoled into doing something that doesn't interest you.

If you enjoy gardening or have a particular artistic passion, then today is the day to indulge!

Gemini Moon

Mutable Air Sign

Today your nemesis is boredom. Its possibility unnerves you. If you were put in a bare room without windows, books, TV, radio, computer, paper or pen, phone, fax, or anything else, you would freak within the hour. This may be true of the other air-sign moons as well, but for the Gemini moon it's a sure thing. Your emotional well-being needs mental stimulation and the means to communicate with others.

It's a good day to start blogging, if you haven't already, to dust off that old manuscript you were working on way back when, or to get together with friends and shoot the breeze. You may feel compelled to sign up for a workshop or even an online course in something that interests you. Or you may decide to go to college or graduate school. It's a great day for research, for delving into a topic or concern and finding out everything you can about it.

Communication, whatever form is takes, is paramount.

Cancer Moon

Cardinal Water Sign

Today your memories work overtime. You're able to conjure sights, smells, tastes, sounds, and textures from your past in vivid detail. The event you're recalling may have happened thirty years ago, but in your memory it's just as fresh and detailed as the day it happened.

The moon rules Cancer, so it's at home in this sign. This is where its energies express themselves most smoothly. Today your emotions are racing through you, and it may be easy to have your feelings hurt. Your acute sensitivity makes you feel vulnerable, and it isn't easy for you to step back and view a situation or relationship dispassionately.

Family, home, and roots are especially important to you today. Schedule time to be with the people you love. Whether it's a traditional family or friends whom you love like family, you draw comfort and sustenance from these individuals. It's a good time to work on creative projects; your inspiration comes from deep places within you. During the Cancer moon you may have a real soft spot for animals—strays that drop by your place for a bowl of food, the neighbor's cat that sneaks into your house. A visit to your local pound may be in order!

Leo Moon

Fixed Fire Sign

It's a perfect day to showcase your talents. In fact when you enter a room, people notice you. If for some reason they don't, you make sure that they do. This isn't just an ego thing, either. Applause and being noticed are vital to your well-being today even if your only audience is your family. *You need to be recognized as someone special.*

Your flair for drama today is remarkable. It runs throughout everything you do—from the way you dress, speak, and act to the activities in which you engage. You may decide to take in a play or try out for a part. Creatively you're at the top of your game, and anything you undertake will bear this dramatic stamp.

It's a good time to spend time with your kids doing something everyone enjoys, volunteer at an animal shelter, get out and be seen, socialize, make new contacts. Network. Be as flamboyant as you can imagine.

Virgo Moon

Mutable Earth Sign

Today you're in a quest for perfection, and the words *Be the best that you can* take on a whole new dimension of meaning. You thrive on order and manage to use today's lunar energy to tackle emotional chaos in your life and impose order on it.

Virgo tends to be a health-oriented sign, so today favors starting a new diet, nutritional program, or exercise regimen. Even if you're already involved in these areas, consider fine-tuning the details. You also may want to consider blogging or writing about what you're learning about health, nutrition, and exercise.

Today also favors performing a service for someone else—not for pay, not with any thought of compensation, but as a good deed. This could mean anything from volunteering at your favorite charity to putting in some time at an animal rescue sanctuary. Pay attention to your spiritual beliefs today. Are you in tune with a greater good? Are your thoughts the most positive they can be?

Libra Moon

Cardinal Air Sign

Among astrologers certain moon signs stir the soul for the sheer beauty of what they represent. The Taurus moon is one of these. The Libra moon is another.

Today at the heart of it you're a lover, a true romantic. Moonlit beaches, bouquets of roses, books of poetry, going to the opera, a summer rain: this is the language your soul speaks during the Libra moon. So first of all surround yourself with beauty today—music, scenery, people. Just the sight of all this beauty will deepen your appreciation for life.

It's a good day for group work—in your community or with your students, peers, or fellow workers. Or it's a great time to socialize and network. Today your interests tend toward people and relationships, your artistic interests, and attaining peace and harmony. You can see both sides of an issue with greater clarity, and try to avoid conflict.

The Libra moon can enhance your intuition, so try to follow your hunches today and see where they lead you. If you don't meditate yet, today is a terrific time to start. It doesn't have to be lengthy. In fact, five minutes in a quiet place, with your mind still, is all you need. You'll come out of it refreshed. Keep track of any impressions that come your way during those five minutes.

If you're in a committed relationship, be sure to take time today to spend time with your partner. Have a romantic dinner at home or at your favorite restaurant. Talk, converse, get in touch with each other.

Scorpio Moon

Fixed Water Sign

Emotionally it's a powerful day. You feel everything so intensely that it's as if some new, inner part of you has awakened from a deep sleep. You may feel as if you've been seized by a force beyond your control. Despite how it feels, this sense of outside forces is just an illusion. Your emotions are your most powerful allies today. They provide you with a direct, immediate connection to the deepest parts of your intuitive self and are capable of instantly transforming your reality.

This transformation happens when you bring your considerable will, intent, and desire to bear against whatever it is that you want to change. When the energy of this moon is focused and backed with passion, this change occurs at the quantum level and can result in the remission of illness or disease, sudden rise in wealth and fame, an explosion of psychic ability . . . well, you get the general idea.

Scorpio is also about power—the power we wield over others and the power others wield over us. All too often this lunar energy is misused or abused when it concerns power issues; then its tremendous capacity for positive transformation becomes negative. The difference seems to be self-awareness.

It's a great day to work with healing energies, intuitive and psychic development, and research and investigation.

Sagittarius Moon

Mutable Fire Sign

Oh, baby, let the good times roll! And for the Sagittarian moon, those good times mean music, deep talk, exotic travel, esoteric ideas. Today you're an explorer. Those explorations may take you to the farther ends of the Earth or deep within the mysteries of the universe. In one way or another this moon enables you to search for the higher truth, the larger picture, a more expansive perspective.

You may be more blunt than usual when dealing with people today, particularly when the other guy just doesn't get what seems so obvious to you. Patience and nuance aren't your strong points during this period. The exception to this occurs when you're pursuing something about which you feel passionate, then you have the patience of Mother Teresa and are as detail oriented as a Virgo.

You're called to action today. You would rather do than think about doing. As a mutable sign, you're emotionally adaptable. You have opinions about virtually everything and aren't the least bit hesitant in expressing these opinions. This becomes a problem if you're dogmatic or bombastic about what you believe and try to convert others to your way of thinking. So today strive to nurture patience and optimism.

Capricorn Moon

Cardinal Earth Sign

The moon isn't particularly comfortable in this sign. It chafes at all the rules and restrictions that Capricorn seeks to impose and dislikes all that earthy grounding. However, this moon certainly favors strategy—laying out goals and figuring ways to achieve them. Your physical energy is excellent today and enables you to work long hours to meet a deadline, regardless of whether that deadline is self-imposed (which it often is) or imposed by a boss.

You feel quite independent today and may find yourself outdoors, hiking alone through the wilderness, or at the gym, putting in extra time on the treadmill. Under this lunar influence you push yourself, move the bar higher, and feel a certain determination to carve your niche in the larger world.

Today it's easier to categorize your emotions, to look at things dispassionately. So tackle stuff that pushes your buttons, issues that you've pushed aside but which beg for a resolution.

Aquarius Moon

Fixed Air Sign

Today you march to a different drummer. You may hear a different kind of music in your very cells and feel compelled to decipher the message and act on it.

This is the sign, after all, that ushers in new paradigms by refusing to go along with the status quo.

The visionary component to this moon sign gives you an edge today on new trends. You can spot the next wave long before anyone else does. The trick is acting on it and putting it to work for you in your personal and professional life. Your rational mind may try to intervene, to argue and put up blocks, to keep you within the confining box of consensus reality. Or someone close to you—a parent, close friend, significant other—inadvertently plays that role, and you suddenly find yourself on the defensive.

So today be fearless; go forward secure in the knowledge that your vision is correct!

Pisces Moon

Mutable Water Sign

Today you're the archetypal dreamer, your feet never really firmly rooted on the earth. You're deeply compassionate today too, a true bleeding heart. You probably won't be able to pass a homeless person on the street without giving him money, and you definitely won't resist the soulful gaze of a stray pup or kitten. Injustices of any sort may fill you with a deep sadness. Your challenge during this moon is to detach emotionally from situations and people who cause you this kind of anguish.

Part of the problem is that today you're a psychic sponge who soaks up the emotions and moods of the people around you. This alone makes it vital that you associate with upbeat, positive people and situations that boost your energy rather than sap it.

The Pisces moon favors imagination, intuition, and any artistic endeavor. On a strictly mundane level it's a fine day to shop for new clothes, get a new hairdo, or redesign yourself in some way. Also, your dreams should be especially vivid and could contain important insights and information.

Eclipses

Every year there are at least four eclipses—two solar, two lunar. Solar eclipses are like double new moons; the opportunities are twice as powerful and delicious. They usually involve external events. Lunar eclipses are about internal events and emotions. Eclipses always come in pairs and form an axis of energy. If there's a solar eclipse in Aries, for example, about two weeks later there will be a lunar eclipse in Libra, the opposite sign of Aries.

When an eclipse falls in your sun, moon, or rising sign, you will feel the effects quite powerfully. Be sure to check out the Big Picture chapter for your sign, where we talk about the year's eclipses.

CHAPTER 6

Mars in 2014

Mars rules fire sign Aries and corules Scorpio. It takes two years to circle the zodiac and spends about two months in a sign. Think of this planet as the action hero of the zodiac, the one who is always on the move, doing, acting, getting things done, your personal warrior.

The sign and house placement for your natal Mars describes how you use your physical energy, your desire for personal achievement, and the nature of your sexuality. First check out one of the astrology sites listed in the book and find out the sign and house placement for your natal Mars. Then find your natal Mars in the descriptions below.

Mars in Aries or in the First House

Since Mars rules this sign, the planet is happy here and functions at optimum levels. If your natal Mars is in Aries, you go after what you want; you are impulsive, sometimes reckless, and basically fearless. You're the one who loves the roller coasters at theme parks and hikes to the summit of Mount Everest and heads out for parts unknown with just a backpack and an ATM card.

You have a need to dominate your immediate environment, and your leadership ability is strong. But sometimes you may lack direction. You're terrific at initiating projects, but if you lose interest, you walk away without regret and leave what you started for someone else to complete.

Your sex drive is particularly strong and can sometimes manifest selfishly, with little regard for your partner. You could be somewhat accident prone.

Mars in Taurus or in the Second House

You aren't easily discouraged by obstacles of any kind. Your sheer determination and strength of will are well developed, but you may not use these attributes to their fullest. You take practical, purposeful action in everything you begin.

You pursue your financial goals with relentless energy and drive, but you may have trouble holding on to what you earn because you enjoy spending. Try to pay cash for your purchases so that you have a clearer grasp of how much money goes out.

Your sexual nature is sensuous, often passionate. You find pleasure through your profession.

Mars in Gemini or in the Third House

Your energy is expressed mentally and intellectually. You're an avid student—even once you're out of school. You tend to take on multiple projects simultaneously, which scatters your energy. Your mental restlessness needs a creative outlet, otherwise you can become argumentative.

You think well on your feet and make decisions quickly. Sometimes you can be so aggressive about communicating your ideas that you create unnecessary tension. With this placement there can be a lot of competition with siblings. Your challenge is to think before you speak. You pursue your goals well, but sometimes have so many goals that your energy is all over the place.

In terms of sexuality your mind has to be courted and seduced first!

Mars in Cancer or in the Fourth House

Your family life is active and emphasizes the development of individuality, competition, and independence. If you feel you have to dominate the domestic scene, that can sometimes be a source of tension.

Your experiences are filtered through a subjective lens. You may be the kind of person who takes everything personally, so it's difficult at times to be objective about issues that are important to you.

The intuitive component with this placement may give you an advantage in terms of your family. You simply have to tune in to find out what your kids are really doing! This intuitive connection also operates with your partner, parents, and anyone else who shares your domestic life.

Your sexuality is particularly heightened when you're emotionally in synch with your partner.

Mars in Leo or in the Fifth House

You're all about passion. It rushes through everything you do and say, even in the way you move. You have strong leadership abilities, are as fearless as Mars in Aries, and your will is powerful and determined. Artistic or musical skills are sometimes indicated with this placement.

You may be into competitive sports, enjoy strenuous physical activity, and are an ardent and considerate lover. You pursue romance and creative endeavors with equal passion, and with both the one thing you should be careful about is acting impulsively.

Your sexuality is powerful, and others pick up on that, so you have no shortage of people clamoring for your attention.

Mars in Virgo or in the Sixth House

Your energy finds expression through efficient, practical pursuits. You're one of the hardest workers around, especially when the work involves attention to details. You dislike laziness in others and may criticize them for it, but that usually gets you nowhere and doesn't change anything.

You pursue your goals with a quiet diligence, rarely giving up or surrendering to despair when something doesn't work out. Sooner or later you attain what you want.

In terms of sexuality you're quite discriminating and picky about what you want in a partner. But once you're smitten, you tend to be loyal.

Mars in Libra or in the Seventh House

Your energy finds its best expression in partnerships and through and with other people. Your marriage and partnerships are infused with energy and are a source of inspiration to you.

You can charm your way into any situation or relationship. You usually understand another person's point of view because you can put yourself in his or her shoes. You excel at diplomacy and seek harmony and peace in whatever you do.

Your sexuality is determined to a large extent on how romantic you feel. It's about *mood*—how your partner approaches you, talks to you, courts you.

Mars in Scorpio or in the Eighth House

Mars corules Scorpio, so the planet is happy here and functions well. Your drive and ambition are legendary among the people who know you. Even strangers notice something about you that's different, out of the ordinary. Your sexuality is important to you, and the intensity with which it's expressed can be intimidating to others.

This same intensity, however, makes you an excellent investigator and researcher. You're never satisfied with easy answers. You dig and dig, always looking for the absolute bottom line in everything you do.

In a marriage or partnership you're actively involved in joint finances. This could cause friction between you and your partner, but it's something you insist on.

This placement for Mars can be quite psychic. At the very least you may delve into metaphysics, experience past-life recall, or see things that others don't.

Mars in Sagittarius or in the Ninth House

Your energy is best expressed in competitive sports, travel, and adventure, and the study of different cultures, philosophies, and spiritual traditions. Mars in Sagittarius can denote a career in publishing or higher education or as a crusader, a New Age leader, or even as an evangelist. You have the courage to act on your convictions.

Your sexuality is passionate but impulsive. You can commit to a relationship, but only when your heart is truly captured. Otherwise you prefer to remain free and unfettered.

Mars in the ninth house often takes wanderlust to new levels. It isn't enough for you to take an annual vacation. You live to travel, explore, and delve into various philosophies and spiritual traditions first hand.

Mars in Capricorn or in the Tenth House

Your energy finds its best expression in your career and profession. You're a worker who sets goals and moves toward them with a strategy, a plan. You're organized and use your time efficiently. When you want something, nothing holds you back. You pursue it with a self-motivation that others find intimidating and remarkable.

You may keep a tight hold on your sexuality. You're guarded and cautious and may get involved with people who are older than you. You have to be deeply certain about a relationship before you commit fully to it.

As a workaholic, it's smart to kick back sometimes

and evaluate where you are and where you're going. You need down times, periods when you relax and recharge.

Mars in Aquarius or in the Eleventh House

Your energy is best expressed through honing your individuality. You participate in groups when those groups support your interests and passions, but otherwise you're a paragon of individuality. Sometimes your approach is so different from the mainstream that others think you're eccentric.

Mars in the eleventh house explores group participation in a deeper way than Mars in other houses. You take the initiative in forming friendships and joining groups, but always there's a purpose behind it. You excel at initiating projects and launching them.

Your sexuality is apt to be unemotional unless you're madly in love with your partner. That said, love and sex begin in the mind for you.

Mars in Pisces or in the Twelfth House

Your energy is primarily intuitive and emotional. You can be inconsistent in the way you try to achieve your goals, or you're able to intuitively pull together facets of a project and make them work.

Your sexuality is intimately tied to your emotions and intuition. The other person has to "feel" right to you; there has to be some sort of heart-centered connection. With Mars in the twelfth house there can be secrecy surrounding your sexuality and relationships.

Sometimes with this placement there's a need to

recognize the ways in which you are aggressive so that the aggression doesn't turn against you and create health problems.

Important Mars and Venus Combinations

If you have a copy of your birth chart, take a look at where both Mars and Venus are located. If they are in the same sign and house, it suggests your sexuality is central to your life. Your passionate nature propels you into many different types of relationships, and not all of them are positive.

Generally this combination indicates that you're extremely attractive to the opposite sex, are fortunate in financial matters, and have artistic ability. It means your passion can be poured into artistic endeavors.

If your natal Mars is three signs away from your natal Venus (Mars in Aries, Venus in Capricorn, for instance), you may find yourself in stormy romances, where you and your partner are rarely on the same page. You may use other people for sexual gratification—or you're used in this way. That's the worst case scenario. However, with a bit of temperance and balance added to the mix, this combination can lead to a relationship in which you maintain your independence, and you and your partner appreciate each other's differences.

When your natal Mars is two signs away from Venus (Mars in Taurus, Venus in Cancer) or four signs away (Mars in Taurus, Venus in Virgo), you get along very well with the opposite sex. Your romantic relationships, partnerships, and marriage are harmonious and satisfying. A lot of your energy goes into creative pursuits.

If your natal Mars is opposite Venus, romantic and sexual relationships can be difficult. You may have to deal with jealousy and other such dark feelings. Your aggression can be intimidating. In extreme cases there can be abuse in relationships.

Everything in your natal chart, however, is indicative only of potential. What you do with that potential is entirely up to you—and your free will.

CHAPTER 7

The Luck Factor in 2014— Synchronicity

The word *synchronicity* was coined by Swiss psychiatrist Carl Jung, when he wrote the introduction to the Richard Wilhelm translation of the *I Ching*. In a nutshell synchronicity is a meaningful coincidence. It happens when inner and outer events come together in a way that is meaningful to the observer and can't be explained by cause and effect.

We've all experienced these events. You're thinking of a friend you haven't seen for years, and suddenly you get an invite from that person on Facebook. Or you're delayed on your way to work one morning, and when you finally arrive at your turnoff discover there was an accident at just about the time you would have driven through if you'd been on time.

Once you're aware that these incidents hold a deeper meaning, they tend to happen more frequently. As you begin to work with these synchronicities, deciphering their messages, you suddenly realize you're in the flow, in the right place at the right time.

The planet that can help us get into the flow— Jupiter—is also the planet that represents luck and expansion, success, prosperity, growth, creativity, spiritual interests, higher education, and the law. It governs publishing, overseas travel, and foreign countries and any of our dealings with them. This year it will be moving through two signs. Between January 1 and July 16 it will be transiting water sign Cancer. Between July 16 and August 11, 2015, it will be moving through fire sign Leo.

Check out www.synchrosecrets.com for a description of the most common types of synchronicities and how to decipher the messages. Sometimes the messages are obvious. But some synchronicities require interpretation. You have to think symbolically.

Now let's take a look at how these transits might attract more synchronicity and luck into your life.

Aries

If you aren't aware of synchronicity, your best time this year for delving into this fascinating phenomenon is between July 16 and August 11, 2015, when Jupiter transits fellow fire sign Leo, your solar fifth house of love, romance, and creativity.

Consider keeping a journal about your experiences as the synchronicities occur. Or create a file on your computer or iPad. Note what types of synchronicity they are. Do they occur in clusters, with the same name, word, or phrase happening repeatedly during a relatively short period of time? Do your experiences act as guidance, confirmation, warning?

It's easy for you to get into the flow, Aries. Just follow your impulses. They often lead you to exactly where you need to be. Or if you have a hunch that you should follow a particular course, by all means follow the hunch. If a dream provides what seems to be information about an issue that concerns you, be sure to consider this information before making a decision.

Jupiter's transit through Leo indicates that you're going to enjoy delving into the topic of synchronicity and that you and a romantic partner may undertake the exploration together. You should experience luck with your creative endeavors, with projects and opportunities coming to you seemingly out of the blue.

Between January 1 and July 16, when Jupiter is transiting Cancer, your luck is heightened when you use your intuition and may involve your home and domestic environment. You might be able to move into a larger home in a neighborhood that suits your family better. Your family might expand—a birth, a parent or relative moves in, a child moves back home. At each step of the way synchronicities may be happening, particularly if major life transitions are occurring.

Taurus

Your luck factor and your synchronicities should be strongest during Jupiter's transit through compatible water sign Cancer: January 1 to July 16. This transit occurs in your solar third house—your neighborhood/ community, siblings and other relatives, education and short-distance travel. These areas of your life may seem particularly lucky, and synchronicities may revolve around these areas.

Since the third house also governs your conscious mind and communication abilities, you may be writing or blogging about your experiences. You might start a Web site or write a book about these experiences.

Consider keeping a journal about your experiences as the synchronicities occur. Or create a file on your computer or iPad. Note what types of synchronicity they are. Do they occur in clusters, with the same name, word, or phrase happening repeatedly during a relatively short period of time? Do your experiences act as guidance, confirmation, warning?

During Jupiter's transit through Leo between July 16, 2014, and August 11, 2015, your luck factor revolves around your home and domestic situation. If you're going through a major transition of some kind—a move, the birth of a child, a change in income—the synchronicities may come fast and furiously.

Gemini

Jupiter's transit through Leo will be the one that is most beneficial for you, your luck factor, and your experience of synchronicity. The dates again: July 16, 2014, to August 11, 2015. It occurs in your solar third house—your neighborhood/community, siblings and other relatives, education and short-distance travel. These areas of your life may seem particularly lucky, and synchronicities may revolve around these areas.

Since the third house also governs your conscious mind and communication abilities, you may be writing or blogging about your experiences. You might start a Web site or write a book about these experiences.

Consider keeping a journal about your experiences as the synchronicities occur. Or create a file on your computer or iPad. Note what types of synchronicity they are. Do they occur in clusters, with the same name, word, or phrase happening repeatedly during a relatively short period of time? Do your experiences act as guidance, confirmation, warning?

Jupiter's transit through Cancer between January 1 to July 16 occurs in your financial area. Expect your financial opportunities to expand tremendously. Your luck factor will revolve around money. Synchronicities will occur in areas where you need guidance, confirmation, or warning.

Cancer

Oh, lucky you! The Jupiter transit to anticipate occurs between January 1 and July 16, when the planet of expansion and luck transits your sign! Everything in your life should expand during this period. Opportunities drop in your lap, your finances probably improve, or you get married or start a new career or family. Your intuition is greatly enhanced during this transit, and you're able to create a rich psychic environment for synchronicity. Be sure to decipher the messages of these synchronicities; they hold valuable information for you.

Consider keeping a journal about your experiences as the synchros occur. Or create a file on your computer or iPad. Note what types of synchronicity they are. Do they occur in clusters, with the same name, word, or phrase happening repeatedly during a relatively short period of time? Do your experiences act as guidance, confirmation, warning?

The second Jupiter transit, through Leo, occurs in

your financial area. This is when your finances really benefit. You land a fat raise, find a new, better-paying job, get a hefty bonus, or pick the right stocks. Synchronicities during this period may revolve around money.

Leo

The first Jupiter transit this year, in Cancer, occurs in your solar twelfth house. The dates: January 1 to July 16.

This period brings heightened insights concerning your own psyche and unconscious. You may try therapy or take up meditation. Jupiter's transit through Cancer makes your unconscious more accessible to you in some way, and you discuss the process with others through a blog or Web site, by writing a book, or keeping a journal. You may even work this process into your professional life in some way. One purpose for this transit is to clear out the old to make way for the new when Jupiter enters your sign on July 16. You may be discarding beliefs that no longer serve your best interests or breaking longstanding habits. Relationships may end but new ones begin.

If you feel this is a period of major transitions for you, the synchronicities are likely to come fast and furiously, offering confirmation, warning, peeks at the future. You might, for instance, dream of someone you know you've never met—only to meet that same person the next day or a week later. Any seeds you sow during this transit will be beneficial down the line, Leo.

During the second transit, when Jupiter is in your

sign, everything in your life opens up. Your luck factor is at its highest, and synchronicities swirl so quickly through your life that you better have a way to record them!

Consider keeping a journal about your experiences as the synchronicities occur. Or create a file on your computer or iPad. Note what types of synchronicity they are. Do they occur in clusters, with the same name, word, or phrase happening repeatedly during a relatively short period of time? Do your experiences act as guidance, confirmation, warning?

Virgo

Between January 1 and July 16 your luck factor and synchronicity experiences revolve around friends, groups to which you belong, your network of friends and acquaintances, and how you can achieve your wishes and dreams. Heady stuff, right?

The contacts you make during this period will be valuable and will expand your dreams in some way. The types of synchronicities you experience could involve virtually anything. The universe has a way of knowing what you need—even if you don't! Be sure to decode the messages that come with these synchronicities; they could prove helpful as guidance and confirmation. Your precision and attention to detail during this time should aid you. Your particular mindset lends itself to solving puzzles and mysteries.

During the second Jupiter transit, which lasts about thirteen months, your personal unconscious expands. This period brings heightened insights concerning your own psyche and unconscious. You may try therapy or take up meditation. Jupiter's transit through Leo and your solar twelfth house makes your unconscious more accessible to you in some way. You may discuss the process with others through a blog or Web site, by writing a book, or keeping a journal. You may even work this process into your professional life in some way.

Libra

During the first six months of the year, while Jupiter transits water sign Cancer and the career area of your chart, your professional life expands tremendously. This period should be exciting, with your professional opportunities multiplying almost more quickly than you can keep up with. You'll be lucky professionally— you're the right person at the right time and place, that sort of lucky. You may change jobs or careers, and if you do, it's for a better position and more pay. You could also be promoted or may decide to launch your own business.

Synchronicity will act as your guide, confirm your hunches, provide warnings or caution, or urge you to move full steam ahead. This period will enable you to make significant professional strides.

The second Jupiter transit, through Leo, occurs between July 16, 2014, and August 11, 2015. It happens in the area of your chart that governs friendships, groups, and your wishes and dreams. The contacts you make during this period will be valuable and expand your dreams in some way. The types of synchronicities you experience could involve virtually anything. The universe has a way of knowing what you need—even if you don't! Be sure to decode the messages that come with these synchronicities; they could prove helpful as guidance and confirmation.

Scorpio

During Jupiter's transit through Cancer, your solar ninth house, between January 1 and July 16 your opportunities and luck factor expand considerably.

The ninth house governs your worldview, higher education, publishing, and foreign travel, so expansions are likely to take place in those areas. Your communication opportunities should expand as well. You might sell a book or novel you've written, go to college or graduate school, or sign up for a seminar or workshop on a topic about which you're passionate. If you travel a great deal during this period, don't be surprised if you begin to experience a flurry of synchronicities.

Your spiritual beliefs will expand too. You may sample different religions or spiritual beliefs, launch a spiritual quest, or even travel to far-flung locales in search of spiritual truths. It all depends, Scorpio, on what you're seeking and how sincere you are in your desires.

Between July 16, 2014, and August 11, 2015, Jupiter transits Leo, your career area, and your professional life expands tremendously. This period should be exciting, with your professional opportunities multiplying almost more quickly than you can keep up with. You'll be lucky professionally—you're the right person at the right time and place, that sort of lucky. You may change jobs or careers, and if you do, it's for a better position and more pay. You could also be promoted or may decide to launch your own business. During this year you have many opportunities to show off your talents and skills.

Consider keeping a journal about your experiences as the synchros occur. Or create a file on your computer or iPad. Note what types of synchronicity they are. Do they occur in clusters, with the same name, word, or phrase happening repeatedly during a relatively short period of time? Do your experiences act as guidance, confirmation, warning?

Sagittarius

Since Jupiter rules your sign, its movements impact you quite personally and powerfully. Between January 1 and July 16 it transits Cancer, your solar eighth house. Your partner's income will expand, and you may be delving more deeply into metaphysics. Your intuitive abilities should deepen considerably under this transit. You may be researching and investigating life after death, communication with spirits, haunted houses, or things that go bump in the night. You'll be fortunate with mundane things as well—mortgages, loans, taxes, insurance, all of which falls under the eighth house. Synchronicities swirl in these areas. You're being guided.

The second transit, between July 16, 2014, and August 11, 2015, occurs in Leo, your solar ninth house. The ninth house governs your worldview, higher education, publishing, and foreign travel, so expansions are likely to take place in those areas. Your communication opportunities should expand as well. You might sell a book or novel you've written, go to college or graduate school, or sign up for a seminar or workshop on a topic about which you're passionate. You'll travel a lot during this period and should experience a flurry of synchronicities.

Your spiritual beliefs will expand too. You may sample different religions or spiritual beliefs, launch a spiritual quest, or even travel to far-flung locales on a spiritual quest of some kind.

Capricorn

During the first six months of the year, while Jupiter transits your opposite sign, Cancer, your partnership opportunities expand tremendously, and there's a strong element of luck to both professional and personal partnerships. You could find exactly the right person for a particular job or as a business partner. You and your partner may decide to move in together or get engaged or married. Be alert for synchronicities in every area of your life, and try to interpret the message and follow the guidance these meaningful coincidences provide.

The second Jupiter transit, between July 16, 2014, and August 11, 2015, occurs in Leo, your solar eighth house. The eighth house dynamics are always intriguing. On one side you have mundane issues—taxes, insurance, bank loans and mortgages—and on the other side you have esoteric stuff—hauntings, life after death, communication with the dead. These issues will be focal points for expansion. Synchronicities are likely to abound in these areas.

It should be easier for you to obtain a mortgage

and bank loan, and you will find yourself drawn to explore things that go bump in the night. You may even travel abroad to investigate crop circles or UFO reports. It all depends on how far outside the box your interests extend.

Aquarius

Between January 1 and July 16 Jupiter transits Cancer, your solar sixth house. The strong intuitive component to this transit helps you make better decisions in your daily work life and in regard to the maintenance of your health. You could land a promotion with more responsibility—and a raise that matches that responsibility—or hire more employees for your company. Regardless, a Jupiter transit usually brings expansion of some kind.

Synchronicities are likely to occur if major life transitions are going on—a move, job or career change, a birth or death in the family, a change in income.

Between July 16, 2014, and August 11, 2015, Jupiter transits Leo, your opposite sign. Your partnership opportunities expand tremendously, and there's a strong element of luck to both professional and personal partnerships. You could find exactly the right person for a particular job or as a business partner. You and your partner may decide to move in together or get engaged or married. Be alert for synchronicities in every area of your life, and try to interpret the message and follow the guidance these meaningful coincidences provide.

Pisces

Jupiter's transit through fellow water sign Cancer between January 1 and July 16 occurs in your solar fifth house—romance, love, creativity! You've got the Midas touch now and synchronicity is your middle name. You may feel you're being led into certain creative endeavors. Luck is on your side. Sounds like a recipe for paradise, doesn't it?

Between July 16, 2014, and August 11, 2015, Jupiter transits Leo, your solar sixth house. This thirteen-month transit should expand your daily work routine and the ways in which you maintain your daily health. You might be promoted, be given more responsibility, and be paid well for it. You might change jobs. However the specifics unfold, you're lucky in this area.

Consider keeping a journal about your experiences as the synchronicities occur. Or create a file on your computer or iPad. Note what types of synchronicity they are. Do they occur in clusters, with the same name, word, or phrase happening repeatedly during a relatively short period of time? Do your experiences act as guidance, confirmation, warning?

CHAPTER 8

Retrograde Planets in 2014

Every planet except the sun and moon experience retrograde motion, when the planet, as viewed from Earth, appears to be moving backward. In astrology a retrograde planet is essentially dormant, like a bear in winter. Its energy is repressed, slower, and often mixed up—as when Mercury, the planet of communication and travel, is retrograde.

During retrograde periods we tend to be less spontaneous, are prompted to think before we speak, and often backtrack through issues, situations, and relationships. We look within. The effect of a retrograde is primarily internal, even though there are many external manifestations of the retrograde.

In 2014 every planet turns retrograde, so let's take a look at when these retrogrades occur and what the effects might be for us.

Mercury

We talk quite a bit throughout the book about Mercury retrograde. It occurs three times a year, for two to three weeks. If you look at the Big Picture chapter for your sign, you'll find a lengthy discussion of Mercury retrograde and what it means for you. So here we're talking generally.

First, Mercury rules both Gemini and Virgo, so the retrogrades may have more of an impact on those two signs. When Mercury turns retrograde, your travel plans go south, there are communication snafus, you miss appointments—or discover you were never on the calendar! If you sign a contract during a Mercury retrograde, the contract may not pan out the way you hoped or the project may fall apart altogether.

In the 2000 presidential election Mercury was retrograde as the election results began to come in. Tom Brokaw announced that Al Gore had won Florida, a critical state for him, and that meant Gore had won the election. But minutes after Mercury turned direct, Brokaw said it was too early to call a winner. Ballot issues were being reported in Palm Beach County. Well, we all know where this one went—straight to the Supreme Court.

Writing now, in early 2012, it looks as if the presidential election is going to have similar issues. On November 6, the day of the election, Mercury turns retrograde in Sagittarius and doesn't turn direct again until November 26. As you read this now in late 2013 or in 2014, you already know how that election turned out!

On a personal level a Mercury retrograde impacts your life according to the sign and natal house in which it falls. Be sure to consult your natal chart as you read through the dates:

February 6 to February 28—retrograde in Pisces. Because it occurs in the early degrees of the sign, Mercury moves back into Aquarius, where it will be when Mercury turns direct again. This means that two areas of your life are affected.

June 7 to July 1—retrograde in Cancer. Again, because it occurs in the early degrees of Cancer, it moves back into Gemini, so two areas of your life are impacted.

October 4 to October 25—retrograde in Scorpio. It begins in the early degrees of Scorpio, slides back into Libra, so once again two areas of your life are affected.

Venus

Venus rules both Taurus and Libra, so they may feel the impact of a Venus retrograde more strongly than other signs. It turns retrograde once every eighteen months or so, and the retrograde period last about six weeks.

When Venus turns retrograde, your love life and finances are often impacted. Relationship issues resurface, and former lovers and spouses may suddenly appear. Friends you haven't heard from in years may get in touch out of the blue. It's an excellent time to reevaluate your closest relationships and decide what you're looking for in a partner.

If you're in a committed relationship, you and your

partner may be sifting back through issues that you thought had been resolved. One or both of you may be distant, emotionally absent, during the retrograde period.

In terms of finances your expenses may increase, and you could feel pinched. The sign and house where Venus falls during the retrograde is important, so be sure to check your natal chart. It's important to avoid buying large-ticket items. That said, however, it's possible to find great deals during a Venus retrograde. One year we bought a used car during a Venus retrograde, only to discover it had been in an accident before we'd bought it. We took it back to the company that sold us the car, and they fixed the problem. We then sold it a year later—for the same price we'd paid for it.

In 2014 Venus is retrograde between January 1 and 31 in Capricorn, a continuation of a retrograde that began in December 2013. Between January 1 and 11 Mercury is traveling with retrograde Venus, which suggests that your focus is strongly on career and professional matters, and you could be discussing things because of some rough patches.

Mars

Mars rules Aries and corules Scorpio, so these two signs may feel the impact of a Mars retrograde most strongly. A Mars retrograde occurs every two years and two months and lasts between fifty-eight to eighty-one days. In 2014 Mars begins the year retrograde in Libra, and that continues until March 1.

During a Mars retrograde your physical energy may not be up to par, so if you're partying every night, not getting enough sleep, pushing against a deadline, eating on the run . . . you may get run down. In other words, take extra good care of yourself during this period.

Mars rules our capacity for physical aggression, how we pursue our ambitions, our sexuality. The retrograde period can prompt you to bottle up anger, which can be detrimental on several levels: the anger festers and then explodes, or it festers and your blood pressure rises, or you get sick. Anger consumes enormous amounts of energy, so you end up feeling exhausted and depressed.

If you're angry at someone in particular, write the person a letter and review every word to make sure you've said exactly what you want to say. Then make a decision about whether to hold onto the letter until Mars turns direct or to give it to the person. Sometimes just writing out what you're feeling defuses the anger.

In terms of your professional life and career, projects and connections may be delayed, don't happen quickly enough, or fall apart midway through the process.

One of the best ways to deal with a Mars retrograde is through physical activity. Be sure to keep up your exercise routine. Or try new forms of exercise — yoga, pilates, brisk walking, running, or playing sports.

Jupiter

Jupiter rules Sagittarius and corules Pisces, so these two signs are apt to feel a Jupiter retrograde more strongly. Jupiter rules travel, luck, speculation, optimism, worldview, philosophy, religion, higher education, and expansion.

For about four months every year it turns retrograde. During this period you're more likely to look within for answers, and it's possible to attain a new level of awareness. You may question issues like self-worth and could be redefining yourself and your values in some way. As your worldview and spiritual beliefs expand, your external life eventually does too.

During a Jupiter retrograde meditation can be enormously beneficial. You're able to center yourself and turn within to find the answers and insights that benefit you. Take a workshop or seminar in intuitive development during the retrograde. Listen to affirmation and visualization tapes.

In 2014 there are two periods when Jupiter is retrograde. Between January 1 and March 6 it's retrograde in Cancer, a continuation of a retrograde that began in November 2013. Then on July 16 Jupiter enters Leo and turns retrograde on December 8. This retrograde lasts until April 8, 2015. Find out where Cancer and Leo fall in your natal chart; those are the areas where the retrograde will affect you most strongly.

Saturn

Saturn rules Capricorn, so when it's retrograde Capricorns are likely to feel the impact strongly. The planet turns retrograde about once a year and remains that way for about four and a half months.

Saturn rules responsibility, obligation, structure, limitations, delays, authority, conservatives, and karma. During the retrograde period everything seems to slow down. You learn how to push through self-imposed limitations because you now have the time to do so. Projects you thought were done deals may be delayed. It's wise not to try to rush things during this retrograde. Strive for what's practical and efficient.

Saturn's energy, direct or retrograde, is difficult to navigate at times. But one way or another we all manage to do so. Keep that in mind during the 2014 retrograde between January 1 and March 6, a continuation of a retrograde that began in 2013. Saturn will be retrograde in Scorpio then, so everything you encounter is likely to have an intense, bottom-line feel to it. Just try to go with the flow, and don't offer resistance!

Uranus

Uranus rules Aquarius, our individuality, sudden, unexpected change, genius, electronics, rebellion, freedom, and revolution. It turns retrograde once a year for about five months.

This planet's job is to awaken us with sudden, unexpected, and jolting events that prompt us to change the things in our lives that no longer work in our best interests. When it's retrograde, you may rebel against the status quo, whatever that is for you, and seek to free yourself from restrictive situations and relationships. You may experience sudden flashes of insight about a concern you have or that illuminates a creative endeavor in which you're involved.

Be sure to check out where Uranus is located in your natal chart. As Uranus retrogrades, you will feel it most strongly when it forms an angle to your natal Uranus or to another planet in your chart.

In 2014 Uranus in Aries is retrograde between July 21 and December 21.

Neptune

Neptune rules Pisces, higher inspiration, illusions, escapism, addiction, creativity, and spirituality. Once a year it's retrograde for about five months.

During this period your inspiration is likely to be powerful, and you'll be able to draw on deep, inner resources for any creative endeavors. Your spiritual beliefs may change or deepen, and you may spend a lot of time reading and studying about various spiritual traditions. It's an excellent period for dream work. Your dreams provide insights, information, and inspiration.

Note where Neptune is in your natal chart, and pay attention to when transiting Neptune is going to form an angle to it or to another natal planet. Neptune often blurs the boundaries between you and other people, so you may have to reestablish those boundaries.

In 2014 Neptune is retrograde in Pisces between June 9 and November 15.

Pluto

Pluto moves at a snail's pace and takes 250 years to circle the zodiac. It rules Scorpio, transformation, human evolution, and everything that is hidden and unseen. In 2014 its retrograde period is from April 14 to September 22.

During this period you have the opportunity to dive into yourself and figure out what's most important to you. Sometimes retrograde periods bring about personal loss and events that are beyond your control. That's how Pluto forces us to evolve and grow, to transform.

If you don't meditate already, start doing it before Pluto turns retrograde. That way the retrograde period may be less jarring for you, and regardless of what happens you'll remain centered and grounded.

Keep Track of Your Retrograde Experiences

During the retrograde of each of the planets this year, keep a record of what you experience. By doing this you build up knowledge about you as impacted by retrograde.

CHAPTER 9

Health Tips for 2014

Why You Take Responsibility

Statistics can be real eye openers. We recently ran across some facts related to health care in the U.S. And they are sobering.

More money per person is spent on health care in the United States than in any other country in the world. Yet life expectancy in this country ranks fiftieth, and the U.S. lags behind other wealthy nations in infant mortality. According to the Institute of Medicine, the United States is the only country in the world that doesn't ensure that all its citizens have health coverage.

When Obama signed the Affordable Care Act into law in 2010, the politically conservative faction screamed that it was socialism. It's not. Socialized medicine is full coverage by the *government*. The mandate in the U.S. was a triumph for private insurance companies, whose bottom line is profit, not health. They will now gain nearly 50 million new clients.

In all fairness, there are some good things about this mandate. Children can be on their parents' insurance policies until the age of twenty-six, and no one can be denied health insurance because of a preexisting condition. Not surprisingly, the mandate has been challenged in court and will come before the Supreme Court in March 2011. You, reading this in 2014, already know the outcome. We don't.

One of the most famous moments in the health care debacle was when an older woman at a Tea Party meeting waved her sign—*No to Obama Care*—while she shouted, "Keep your hands off my Medicare!"

You know, Medicare, the *government-run* insurance program for people sixty-five and older. Medicare for all should have been implemented, not mandated by health insurance.

Until insurance companies are removed from health care, the health care in this country will continue to be a discriminatory system. The real death panels will continue to be insurance companies who deny care for profit.

If nothing else, that debate and the reality of health care in this country should encourage you to take charge of your own health. Here are some simple suggestions:

1) *If you don't have a regular exercise routine yet, start one.* Pick something that you know you can do daily.

2) *Watch what you eat. Read the labels on the food you buy.* How much sodium is there in your favorite foods? How much cholesterol? Fats? Even organic foods have a high sodium content. The other day at Whole Foods we picked up some soy bacon and then

turned the box over to look at the contents. For a single slice of soy bacon, the nutritional facts state:

Total fat—1 gram
No saturated or trans fat, no polyunsaturated or monounsaturated fats
Cholesterol—0 mg
Sodium—140 mg
Potassium—40 mg
No carbs, no sugar
Protein—2 g

That's a lot of sodium for a single skinny slice of soy bacon! Compare this to our favorite organic chicken sausage, however, which has 460 mg of sodium for a single link, and the soy bacon looks good. Once you get into the habit of reading the labels, you will be more careful in your selection of foods.

3) *Meditation and yoga are two healthy practices you might consider*. Meditation has been shown to: lower blood pressure and oxygen consumption, decrease respiratory rate, slow heart rate, reduce anxiety and stress, and enhance the immune system. Yoga increases your physical flexibility—and eventually your emotional and mental flexibility as well. It helps to strengthen your body, improves muscle tone, improves posture, improves lung capacity because of the deep breathing involved, and reduces stress.

4) *Try various nutritional and vitamin programs*. Educate yourself. The Internet is filled with health and fitness Web sites.

5) *Try a homeopathic practitioner or acupuncturist before you run to your doctor for a prescription*.

If you were an alien watching the evening news and the drug commercials that sponsor it, you might get the impression that Americans are a sickly lot in search of the quickest fix. While drugs certainly have their place, more and more Americans are seeking alternative treatments for whatever ails them. From acupuncture to yoga and homeopathy, from vitamin regimens to nutritional programs, more of us are taking control over our own health and bodies.

6) *Take inventory of your beliefs.* If medical intuitives like Louise Hay, Carolyn Myss, and Mona Lisa Schultz are correct, our health is about more than just eating right and getting sufficient exercise. It's also about our emotions, inner worlds, and belief systems. How happy are you in your job? Your closest partnerships? Your friendships? Are you generally happy with the money you earn? What would you change about your life? Do you believe you have free will or that everything is destined? Is your mood generally upbeat? Do you feel you have choices? Do you feel empowered? By asking yourself these kinds of questions, you can glean a sense of your emotional state at any given time. And the state of your emotions may tell you a great deal about the state of your health.

7) *Forgive yourself and others.* Resentment that you keep bottled up inside you for months or even years can adversely affect your health. It's why medical intuitives and holistic physicians recommend practicing the art of forgiveness. It's not easy to forgive people who have hurt you, but once you're able to forgive them, you're releasing resentment.

8) *Practice the art of appreciation. Expect the best from others.* If you can get into the habit of doing

these two things, you're well ahead of the game in maintaining your health.

The Physical You

These descriptions fit both sun and rising signs. For a more complete look at the physical you, of course, your entire natal chart should be taken into account, with a particularly close look at the sign of your moon—the root of your emotions, the cradle of your inner world.

Aries

Rules: Head and Face

2014 Tip:

In this year of the new you try something new in the way you care for yourself and your health.

Health and Fitness

Aries rules the head and face, so these areas are often the most vulnerable physically. Headaches, dizziness, and skin eruptions can be common. If you're an athletic Aries, do more of whatever it is that you enjoy. Competitive sports? Great, go for it. Long distance runner? Run farther. Gym? Double your time and your workout. Yoga once a week? Do it three times a week. One way or another, you need to burn off your excessive energy so that it doesn't turn inward and short-circuit your body!

As a cardinal fire sign, you're an active person who gravitates toward daring, risky sports—mountain climbing, rappelling, bungee jumping, trekking through high mountainous regions, leaping out of airplanes. It's probably a great idea to have good health insurance or to have a Louise Hay attitude toward your health—*I'm attracting only magnificent experiences into my life.*

For maximum benefit, you probably should try to eliminate red meat from your diet. Chicken and fish are fine, but a vegan diet would be best. Herbs like mustard, eye-bright, and bay are beneficial for you. Any antioxidant is helpful—particularly vitamins C, E, A, or Lutein for your eyes, zinc, Co-Q10, Black Cohosh if you're a female in menopause, or Saw Palmetto if you're a man older than fifty. If you pull a muscle or throw your back out of whack, look for a good acupuncturist and avoid pain killers.

In this year of the new you, practice what you learned last year to transform yourself from the inside out. Start with your thoughts. Notice what you think throughout a given day. If you notice that a lot of negative thoughts surface, nudge them on their way by reaching for more positive ones.

Taurus

Rules: Neck, Throat, Cervical Vertebrae

2014 Tip:

In this year of the new you, reach out to strangers, join a group of like-minded individuals, and keep expressing your feelings. Blogging is one excellent way to do that.

Health and Fitness

Thanks to the sensuality of your sign, you may be a gourmet cook and enjoy rich foods. But because your metabolism may be somewhat slow, you benefit from daily exercise and moderation in your diet. In fact, moderation in all things is probably a good rule to follow.

As a fixed earth sign, you benefit from any outdoor activity, and the more physical it is, the better it is for you. Hiking, skiing, windsurfing, biking are all excellent pursuits. You also benefit from any mind/body discipline like tai chi or yoga. The latter is especially good since it keeps you flexible, and that flexibility spills over into your attitudes and beliefs and the way you deal with situations and people. You probably enjoy puttering in a garden, but because you have such an artistic side, you don't just putter. You remake the garden into a work of art—fountains, bold colors, mysterious paths that twist through greenery and flowers. Once you add wind chimes and bird feeders, nature's music adds the finishing touches.

If your job entails long hours of sitting in front of a computer, your neck and shoulders may be more tense than usual. You would benefit through regular massage and hot tub soaks.

If you're the silent type of Taurus, then chances are you don't discuss your emotions. This tendency can cause health challenges if you keep anger or resentment bottled up inside you. Best to have an outlet—through exercise, for example, or through some sort of creative endeavor. Art, music, photography, writing—

any of those would help. Better yet, learn to open up with at least one or two people!

Gemini

Rules: Hands, Arms, Lungs, Nervous System

2014 Tip:

In this year of the new you, practice focusing on one thing at a time. Don't spread yourself too thinly.

Health and Fitness

You benefit from periodic breaks in your established routine. Whether it's a trip to some exotic port or a trip to the grocery, it's a breath of fresh air, a way to hit the pause button on your busy mind. Regular physical exercise helps to bleed off some of your energy and keeps your already youthful body supple and in shape.

As a mutable air sign, you need intellectual stimulation and a constant array of experiences and information to keep your curiosity piqued. Otherwise it's too easy for all that nervous energy to turn inward and affect your health. The kind of work you do is important in the overall scheme of your health. You do best in nonroutine kinds of work with flexible hours or, preferably, in a profession where you make your own hours! Any job in communication, travel, public relations, would suit you. When you're passionate about what you do, you're happier. If you're happy, your immune system remains healthy.

With your natural dexterity and coordination, you

would do well at yoga. If you don't take classes yet, sign up for some. Not only will they keep you flexible, but you'll benefit mentally. Meditation would also be an excellent practice for you. Anything to calm your busy head!

Since your respiratory and nervous systems are your most vulnerable areas, your diet should include plenty of fish, fresh fruits, and vegetables. If you live in a place where you can garden, then plant some of these items in a garden for optimum freshness. Vitamin C, zinc, the B vitamins, and vitamins E and A are also beneficial for you. With your energy always in fast-forward, it's smart to get at least seven and preferably eight hours of sleep a night. If you're the type of Gemini with a high metabolism, you benefit from eating several small meals throughout the day rather than just the usual three.

Cancer

Rules: Breasts, Stomach, Digestive System

2014 Tip:

During this year of the new you, practice being more objective.

Health and Fitness

As a cardinal water sign, you benefit from proximity to water. If you can live or work close to a body of water, you'll notice a marked difference in your energy and intuition and how you feel and think. Even a vacation close to it is healing. This seems to hold true not only for Cancer sun signs, but for moon and rising signs in Cancer too. The body of water can be anything—a lake, river, ocean, salt marsh, even a pond!

Not surprisingly, you benefit from any kind of water sport, even a day at the beach or a picnic by the river. The point is that water speaks to you. It feels like your natural element. You might want to read *The Secret of Water* or any of the other books by Masaru Emoto. You will never think of water in the same way again and will be more conscious of how human emotions affect water—and thus our bodies, since we consist of nearly 70 percent water.

Emotionally you may cling to past injuries and hurts more than other signs or may still be dragging around issues from childhood or even from a past life. Unresolved emotional stuff can lodge in your body and create problems. So it's important that you rid yourself of past resentments and anger. Use hypnosis to dislodge these feelings. Forgive and forget. Have a past-life regression. Read Louise Hay's book *You Can Heal Your Life.*

If you have a moon, rising, or another planet in an earth sign, consider regular workouts at a gym.

Leo

Rules: Heart, Back, Spinal Cord

2014 Tip:

In this year of the new you, keep drama to a minimum. Whenever you feel yourself at the brink of an emotional outburst or meltdown, detach, step back.

Health and Fitness

Leo rules the heart. So you benefit from a low-fat diet, exercise, work that you love, and relationships in which you are recognized as the unique person that you are. Yes, those last two things count in the overall picture of your health!

Let's talk about your work. Acting, of course, is what you're known for. And performance. And politics. And, well, anything where you can show off your abundant talents. So if right now you're locked into a humdrum job, low person on the bureaucratic totem pole, and don't receive the attention you feel you deserve, then your pride and ambition are suffering. That, in turn, creates resentment that could be eating you alive. Turn the situation around by finding a career or an outlet where your talents shine and you're appreciated and recognized. You're a natural leader whose flamboyant style and magnetism attract the supporters who can help you.

You have a temper, but once you blow, that's it. Unlike Cancer, you don't hold on to grudges or harbor resentments or anger from childhood. You tend to be forward looking in your outlook, and your natural optimism is healthy for your heart and immune system. Anything you can do to maintain your cheerful disposition is a plus. When you feel yourself getting down, rent comedies, find books that make you laugh out loud, blog about your feelings.

Virgo

Rules: Intestines, Abdomen, Female Reproductive System

2014 Tip:

Since this is the year of the new you, stick to your exercise routine. Do it regularly. And strive not to be self-critical.

Health and Fitness

If you're the type of Virgo who worries and frets a lot, the first place it's likely to show up is in your digestive tract. You might have had colic as an infant, stomach upsets as a teenager, ulcers as an adult. The best way to mitigate this tendency, of course, is to learn how NOT to worry and to simply go with the flow.

You do best on a diet that includes plenty of fresh fruits and vegetables, fish, and chicken. Try to stay away from fried or heavily spiced foods. Red meat might be difficult to digest. If you live in a place where fresh fruits and vegetables are difficult to find during the winter, supplement your diet with the appropriate vitamins and minerals. If you're a fussy eater—and some Virgos are—the vitamin and mineral supplements are even more important.

You benefit from hot baths, massages, anything that allows you to relax into the moment. Yoga, running, swimming, gym workouts—any of these exercise regimens benefit you. Some Virgos, particularly double Virgos—with a moon or rising in that sign—have an acute sense of smell. If you're one of those, be sure to treat yourself to scented soaps and lotions, fragrant candles and incense, and any other scent that soothes your soul.

Virgo is typically associated with service, and you may find that whenever you do a good deed for someone, when you volunteer your time or expertise, you feel better about yourself and life in general. The more you can do to trigger these feelings, the healthier you'll be. You have a tendency toward self-criticism that's part and parcel of your need for perfection, and whenever you find yourself shifting into that critical frame of mind, stop it in its tracks. Reach for a more uplifting thought. This will help you to maintain your health.

Libra

Rules: Lower Back, Kidney, Diaphragm

2014 Tip:

During this year of the new you, try not to bend over backward to please the people in your life.

Health and Fitness

If your love life is terrific, then your health probably is too. You're happiest when you're in a relationship, preferably a committed, lifetime relationship. When things between you and your partner are on an even keel, your energy is greater, your immune system works without a hitch, you sleep more soundly, and you're more apt to have a healthier lifestyle.

You prefer working in an environment that's aesthetically pleasing, where there's a minimum of drama, and with congenial people. If your work situation doesn't fit that description, it could affect your health—and for the same reason as a love life that is lacking—emotions. Your lower back, kidneys, and diaphragm are vulnerable areas for you and unvented emotions could manifest in those areas first. If it isn't possible to change jobs or careers right now, then find an artistic outlet for your creative expression. Music, photography, art, writing, dance, any area that allows you to flex your creativity.

You benefit from yoga, walking, swimming, and any kind of exercise that strengthen your lower back muscles. Meditation is also beneficial, particularly when it's combined with an awareness of breathing.

The healthiest diet for you should consist of foods with varied tastes, plenty of fresh fruits and vegetables, organic if possible, and a minimum of meats. Anything that benefits your kidneys is good. Drink at least eight glasses of water a day, so that your kidneys are continually flushed out.

Scorpio

Rules: Sexual Organs, Elimination

2014 Tip:

In this year of the new you, listen closely to your intuition, particularly in health matters.

Health and Fitness

As a fixed water sign, you probably benefit by a proximity to water every bit as much as Cancer does. Lake, ocean, river, ocean, pond, salt marsh—take your pick. If none of these is available, put a fountain in your backyard or somewhere in your house, and create a meditation area. It's important that you have a quiet center where you can decompress at the end of the day, particularly if you have a busy family life and a lot of demands on your time.

You tend to keep a lot of emotion locked inside, and if the emotions are negative—resentment, anger—they fester and affect your health. So try to find someone you can talk to freely about your emotions—a partner, friend, family member. Or pour these feelings into a creative outlet. One way or another, get them out.

Scorpio rules the sexual and elimination organs, so these areas could be where ill health hits first. Be sure that you eat plenty of roughage in your diet and enjoy what you eat, while you're eating it. Stay away from the usual culprits—fried or heavily processed foods. You do best with plenty of fresh food, but may want to consider eliminating red meats. Consider colonic treatments for cleaning out the bowels.

For your overall health, it's important to enjoy sex with a partner whom you trust. Avoid using sex as a leverage for power in a relationship.

Sagittarius

Rules: Hips, Thighs, Liver

2014 Tip:

The new you in 2014 is a person who commits to a healthy lifestyle.

Health and Fitness

As a mutable fire sign, you can't tolerate any kind of restriction or limitation on your freedom. You must be able to get up and go whenever you want. If you work in a job that demands you punch a time clock, where your hours are strictly regulated, or are in a relationship where you feel constricted, you probably aren't happy. For a naturally buoyant and happy person like you, that could spell health challenges. Sadge rules the hips, the sacral region of the spine, the coccygeal vertebrae, the femur, the ileum, the iliac arteries, and the sciatic nerves, so any of these areas could be impacted health-wise.

You benefit from any kind of athletic activity. From competitive sports to an exercise regimen you create, your body craves regular activity. You also benefit from yoga, which keeps your spine and hips flexible.

If you're prone to putting on weight—and even if you're not!—strive to minimize sweets and carbs in your diet. The usual recommendations—abundant fresh vegetables and fruits—also apply. If you're the type who eats on the run, you may be eating fast or heavily processed foods and should try to keep that to a minimum or eliminate it altogether. Even though your digestive system is hardy enough to tolerate just about anything, the fast foods and processed foods add carbs and calories.

Antioxidants are beneficial, of course, and these include vitamins C, A, and E. Minerals like zinc should be included in your diet and also a glucosamine supplement for joints.

Capricorn

Rules: Knees, Skin, Bones

2014 Tip:

The new you understands the value of relaxation and doing what you enjoy.

Health and Fitness

Since you seem to have been born with an innate sense of where you're going—or want to go—it's likely that you take care of yourself. You know the routine as well as anyone—eat right, stay fit, exercise, get enough rest. But there are other components to living long and prospering (to paraphrase Spock!). And that's your emotions.

You, like Scorpio, are secretive, although your motives are different. For you it's a privacy factor more than anything else. You keep your emotions to yourself and may not express what you feel when you feel it. This can create blockages in your body, notably in your joints or knees. It's vital that you learn to vent your emotions, to rid yourself of anger before it has a chance to move inward.

You're focused, ambitious, and patient in the attainment of your goals. But your work—your satisfaction with it—is a primary component in your health. If you feel you've reached a dead end in your career, if you're frustrated more often than you're happy with what you do, it's time to revamp and get out of Dodge. By taking clear, definite steps toward something else, you feel you're more in control of your destiny and mitigate the possibility of health challenges.

Since your knees are vulnerable, running is probably not the best form of exercise for you, unless you do it only once or twice a week and engage in some other form of exercise the rest of the time. For a cardio workout that isn't as tough on your knees, try a rowing machine. For general flexibility, there's nothing like yoga!

Aquarius

Rules: Ankles, Shins, Circulatory System

2014 Tip:

In this year of the new you, Aquarius, you maintain your exercise routine. No more cheating!

Health and Fitness

Let's start with the effect of Uranus ruling your sign. It sometimes can set your nerves on edge—too many sounds, too much chaos around you, loud noises deep into the night, the backfiring of cars, the incessant drone of traffic, even a crowd at the local mall. You're sensitive to all of that. It's part of what makes it important for you to have a private space to which you can withdraw—a quiet back yard filled with plants, a room inside your house with an altar for your Wiccan practice, filled with scents from candles or incense that soothe your frazzled nerves. Or perhaps a book on tape can shut it all out. But shut it out you must to protect your health.

Because you live so much inside your own head, exercise is definitely beneficial for you. It doesn't have to be anything complicated—yoga done in the privacy of your own home, long walks, regular bike rides. But do *something* to ground your body, to get your blood moving, to silence the buzz inside your head. It will all benefit your health.

Nutrition? Well for an Aquarian this can go any number of different ways. You enjoy different types of food, so that's a place to start—with what you *enjoy*. The foods are likely to be unusual—organically grown, for instance, prepared in unusual ways, or purchased from a local co-op. If you live in the city, perhaps you purchase food from a grocery store you've been frequenting for years. The idea here is that *you* know what's best for your body, what you can tolerate, what you need. Even though Aquarians aren't generally as in touch with their bodies as earth signs, they have an intuitive sense about what works for them. In the end that's all that matters.

Pisces

Rules: Feet, Lymphatic System

2014 Tip:

The new you treats yourself as you treat others.

Health and Fitness

Let's start with emotions. Let's start with the fact that you're a psychic sponge, able to absorb other people's moods and thoughts with the ease of a magnet attracting every other piece of metal around it. Yes, let's start there. It's why you should associate only with optimistic, upbeat people. The negative types steal your energy, wreck your immune system, and leave you in a tearful mess at the end of the rainbow with nothing to show for your journey.

Like your fellow water signs Cancer and Scorpio, you probably benefit from proximity to water. Whether you live near water, work near it, or vacation near it, water refreshes your soul, spirit, intuition, and immune system. Read Masaru Emoto's books on how water responds to emotions and intent. You'll never think about water in the same way again. You'll never think about your sun sign in the same way again either.

You benefit from any kind of exercise, but try something that speaks to your soul. Swimming. Rowing, but in an actual boat, on an actual river instead of in a gym. Even a hot tub where you kick your legs is beneficial. Pay attention to the water you drink. Is your tap water filled with fluorides? Then avoid it, and look for distilled water. Drink at least eight glasses a day. Indulge yourself in massages, foot reflexology, periodic dips in the ocean. Any ocean.

CHAPTER 10

Your Creativity in 2014

We're innately creative beings who reinvent ourselves constantly. From our appearances to the way we work to our interactions with others, we rarely repeat the same action in exactly the same way. In 2014 it's important that we use our creativity to solve problems and meet challenges in our work, careers, and relationships.

Due to rapidly changing technology, some of us may need to reinvent ourselves professionally. With the popularity of ebooks, for instance, the publishing industry is no longer as centralized as it once was. Writers can now self-publish through any number of services and link their books to Amazon. Artists or photographers who once had to haul around portfolios can now have digital portfolios. Actors and actresses who once had to carry around scripts while learning their lines can now use iPads to view their lines.

How can you use your creativity to redefine yourself this year? Let's take a look.

Aries

As a natural trailblazer and entrepreneur, you have no trouble coming up with new ideas about how to reinvent yourself. Your challenge, though, is carrying through from beginning to end.

The carry-through may be easier for you to accomplish while Jupiter is in fellow fire sign Leo, between July 16, 2014, and August 11, 2015. Jupiter helps you to expand your ideas, to develop your creativity to the point where it becomes second nature. You also have Uranus in your sign helping you to get rid of whatever has gone stale in your life.

So during 2014 don't hesitate to think outside the box, take professional and emotional risks, and follow impulses. It's your path to embracing change.

Taurus

As a fixed earth sign, you are slow to change. You tend to hold on to clothes you no longer wear, jobs that don't suit you, relationships that you've outgrown. In any area where you feel dissatisfaction this year, take a closer look and try to determine if your feelings are transitory, just a mood, or whether it's something more than that. If your dissatisfaction is genuine, how can you change things around?

If your job is the problem, perhaps there are additional skills you can learn and credentials you can garner that will enable you to land a better job that is more suited to your temperament and in a field you love. That's the point here: change that you enjoy, that helps you to evolve creatively.

Develop a strategy, and then use your resoluteness to make it work. This process will be easier for you between January 1 and July 16, while Jupiter transits compatible water sign Cancer and expands your intuition.

Gemini

Change is your middle name. Your challenge, though, is that you sometimes change so rapidly that you aren't sure who you are when you get up in the morning. It's why your sign depicts twins!

In 2014 use your adaptability and innate creativity to focus on one particular area in your life that you would like to change—job, career, relationships, finances. Whatever the area is, decide what you want, how you might best attain it, and then pursue it. If you're the kind of Gemini who enjoys writing, consider blogging about your experiences. You never know how it may help or influence someone else.

Your best time for initiating change and using your creativity to bring it about falls between July 16, 2014, and August 11, 2015, when Jupiter transits compatible fire sign Leo. During this period you're on a creative roll.

Cancer

You're usually so in touch with your feelings that you know when dissatisfaction is just a passing mood and when it addresses something deeper. So take that area of your life where you're feeling genuine dissatisfaction and try to see it objectively. That may be a challenge for you, Cancer. You tend to view the world through a subjective lens, but in this instance objectivity will serve you better.

Once you've identified whatever it is you want to change, use your prodigious intuition to figure out how to initiate the change. Use dream recall, meditation, visualization, and the other intuitive tools you possess. Then act on that information, trusting that your guidance will bring about what you desire.

Synchronicities may proliferate during this process, so be sure to decipher the messages, these signs and symbols that lead you through the unknown. This process will be greatly facilitated between January 1 and July 16, when Jupiter transits your sign.

Leo

Like your fixed-sign cousin Taurus, you're not crazy about change. You like things the way they are, thank you very much. Yet when you feel a deep dissatisfaction about something in your life, you certainly have the creative abilities to initiate change and transform your job, relationships, finances, whatever it is.

As Jupiter transits your sign between July 16, 2014, and August 11, 2015, there will be a lot of changes. This planet seeks to expand your life and creative abilities and ushers in the opportunities for doing so. Your challenge will be to avoid drama and just get on with it.

Jupiter's transit through Cancer from January 1 to July 16 will enable you to hone in on beliefs and attitudes that may be holding you back. Once you understand the origin of these beliefs, you can use them as creative fodder, so they are really illuminated to your conscious mind, and change them. Then you can change those beliefs, and your life will change accordingly.

Virgo

You, like your mutable cousin Gemini, welcome change. But you prefer it to occur on your terms, in your time frame, according to your specifications; in other words, when you're ready for it. But because you share the planet with seven billion other souls, change often happens on its own, and then you have to adapt quickly to the new circumstances. You have a plethora of creative talents that enable you to do this.

Your creativity, in fact, is central to who you are. Whether change is something you initiate, or it comes about due to global events, your creativity kicks in, and you're able to move with the flow. Your creativity is apt to be enormously powerful between January 1 and July 15, when Jupiter transits compatible water sign Cancer.

During this transit your intuition expands, and you're able to tap deep creative reservoirs in your being. Don't fritter away this opportunity for personal and professional growth.

Libra

You, like your cardinal cousins Aries and Cancer, are a focused individual and aren't fond of change that is thrust upon you. But when that happens, your creative talents rush in to help you sort things out, and you're able to use the change to your advantage.

If there's some area of your life where you feel dissatisfied, bring your enormous focus to bear on changing it. Don't concentrate on what's wrong, but on the end result you want. See it vividly in your mind—a new you, more money, a better job, a relationship. Whatever it is, imagine it and back that image with emotion.

Your best time for making things happen occurs during Jupiter's transit of compatible fire sign Leo between July 16, 2014, and August 11, 2015.

Scorpio

Your creativity is legendary among the people who know you, and in 2014 it could become legendary to the rest of the world too. You, like your fixed cousins Taurus and Leo, tend to be quite stubborn about how to do something. In 2014 this stubbornness serves you well when it comes to your creative endeavors. You know for an end product, so stick to what you know. However, be open to suggestions by other creative people.

If there are areas of your life that beg for change, shed the stubbornness, delve deeply into your intuitive ability, and figure out what your ideal is. Then listen to your intuition about how to attract the ideal into your life.

This process will be easier when Jupiter is in fellow water sign Cancer between January 1 and July 16.

Sagittarius

You enjoy change, as long as it doesn't restrict your freedom. After all, the source of your creativity is that very freedom you savor, which is as necessary to your life as oxygen.

If there is a particular area of your life that dissatisfies you, it's time to hit the road, Sadge, and allow your creativity to come up with options, solutions, answers, a strategy. Your muse will come out of hiding as soon as you're traveling, and then it's up to you to listen closely, interpret, and create.

Your best time for engaging this process is when Jupiter transits fellow fire sign Leo between July 16, 2014, and August 11, 2015.

Capricorn

You're a focused, self-directed individual who wants life to be grounded, tangible, and unfold one step at a time. You usually know when something in your life is *off,* but may not know how to correct it. That's when your creativity sweeps in and discovers the options, solutions, the new path.

During Jupiter's transit of Cancer, your opposite sign, between January 1 and July 16 your intuition deepens and becomes one of your staunchest allies. A family member or partner—business or romantic—may prove helpful in changing something essential in your life.

The beauty of Capricorn's energy is simple. You steadily climb the mountain toward your goal, and when you encounter a block, you search for and usually find an alternate path to wherever you're going.

Aquarius

You and your fixed-sign cousins — Taurus, Leo, Scorpio — aren't fond of change. But you understand that change is inevitable, that it's the only constant, and so you embrace it as you do most things in life, with your intellect. Once you grasp the core of what's happening, you allow yourself to feel your way through it.

You're a visionary, and your creativity reflects that. You're able to spot a trend long before it reaches a tipping point and use that knowledge and foresight to transform any area of your life with which you're dissatisfied. The best time to tackle this process is when Jupiter transits Leo, your opposite sign, between July 16, 2014, and August 11, 2015.

During this period your business and personal partnerships expand, you have a chance to demonstrate your creative abilities, and a partner is instrumental in helping you to create a life that suits you in every way.

Pisces

You and your mutable cousins — Gemini, Virgo, and Sagittarius — are best equipped to deal with change. But for you any kind of change requires an emotional adjustment, and this is where things can get dicey.

You are in touch with your emotions, so you know when something is off kilter. But you may not know how to change whatever it is. This is when your powerful imagination comes into play. Whatever you can imagine and back with emotion can be brought into your life. Allow your creativity to explore your options. Be innovative.

For you Jupiter's transit through fellow water sign Cancer will be the best time to experiment. The dates: January 1 to July 16.

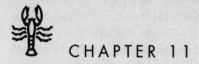

CHAPTER 11

Aspects

An aspect is the angle that planets make to other planets in a natal chart—by transit, progression, solar return, or any other system in astrology. For the purpose of this book, we primarily look at where these transiting planets hit your solar houses and the angles they make to your sun and each other. Some of these angles are beneficial, others are challenging. Think of aspects as a symbolic network of arteries and veins that transports the blood of astrology. In a natal chart these angles connect our inner and outer worlds, accentuate certain traits, and play down others. Each aspect represents a certain type of energy, so there really aren't any good or bad aspects because energy is neutral. It's what we do with the energy that counts. It comes back to free will. When transiting planets make angles to each other and to our natal planets, energy is also exchanged.

For instance, every year there is at least one very lucky day when the transiting sun and transiting Jupiter form a beneficial angle to each other—a conjunction (same sign and degree), a sextile (60 degrees apart), or a trine (120 degrees apart). In 2014 there are two such dates—July 25–26, when the sun and Jupiter are conjunct. This means that the sun's life energy and Jupiter's expansive energy combine and create, well, some magic for all of us! It's especially good for Leo and other fire signs. But since we all have Leo somewhere in our charts, these two days are lucky for the rest of us too.

If you look back to the presidential election in November 2008, Saturn in Virgo and Uranus in Pisces formed an exact opposition to each other. They were 180 degrees apart, an aspect that is like a tug-of-war. In this case the tug-of-war was between the candidate that represented the old paradigm, the established order—Saturn—and the candidate who symbolized sweeping change—Uranus.

Aspects are most powerful as they are approaching exactness. So even though a conjunction, for example, is 00 degrees of separation or a square is technically 90 degrees of separation, many astrologers use *orbs* that can be as wide as 5 or 10 degrees. Some astrologers use small orbs, but others assign larger orbs for the sun and moon and smaller orbs for other planets. The closer the orb, the more powerful the combination. If you're sensitive to transits, then, you may be feeling lucky for several days before and after July 25–26.

In terms of a natal chart, any transiting planet that is approaching an aspect with one of your natal planets is also most powerful on its approach. The traditional aspects have been used since the second century A.D. They are the conjunction, sextile, square, trine, and opposition. These aspects are considered to be the major or hard angles and are also the most power-ful. There are other minor aspects that astrologers use, but for the purpose of this chapter, we'll only talk about the traditional aspects.

Conjunction, Major Hard Aspect, 0 Degrees

This aspect is easy to identify—clusters of planets within a few degrees of each other, usually but not always in the same sign and house. But it's a complex aspect because energies combine, fuse, merge. Think of it as power and intensity, and that's true whether it's in your natal chart or is a transiting planet con-juncting your sun sign. If you have conjunctions in your natal chart, the astrologer who reads for you should address what it means and how you can use it to maximize your potential.

Sextile, Major Soft Aspect, 60 Degrees

Planets that are sextile to each other flow well to-gether, feed each other. According to house and sign, they may confer artistic ability, the gift of gab, greater imagination, higher intuition.

Square, Major Hard Aspect, 90 Degrees

Friction, angst, *oh my God, the sky is falling*: that's how squares feel in a natal chart. The sky, of course, is never falling, but the friction and angst are quite real and act as triggers for action and forward thrust. They force us to develop, evolve, and reach aggressively for our desires.

Trines, Major Soft Aspect, 120 Degrees

This aspect works like a sextile, linking energies in a harmonious way. It's associated with general ease and good fortune, and it means the same whether it's in the natal chart or by transit. People with a lot of trines in their natural charts are sometimes at a disadvantage because things come so easily to them.

Opposition, Major Hard Aspect, 180 Degrees

This aspect feels like a persistent itch that you can't reach and usually involves polarities—Taurus/Scorpio, for example, or Aries/Libra. It brings about change through conflict and sometimes represents traits we project onto others because we haven't fully integrated them into ourselves. Again the opposition applies to transits as well as to natal planets.

When checking the transits in your own chart, always keep in mind the meanings of the two planets involved, the meanings of the houses, and the meanings of the aspects.

Some other minor aspects that astrologers use are:

- the semi-square, 45 degrees. It creates irritation and friction between the planets involved.
- the septile, 51 degrees. Indicative of harmony and union in a nontraditional way. Can suggest spiritual power.
- the quincunx or inconjunct, 150 degrees separation. Indicates a need for adjustment in attitude and beliefs.

CHAPTER 12

The Astrological Neighborhood

Several years ago a Google search for the word *astrology* turned up about 40 million links. Today a Google search results in 114 million links. It suggests that as greater numbers of people search for information and insights, astrology has exploded in popularity.

You can find sites for virtually any aspect of this fascinating field, but some sites are far superior and more user friendly than others. These sites offer free natal charts, daily transits, monthly horoscopes, and political and world predictions. It's all at your fingertips. We have a blog at www.sydneyomarr.blogspot .com. In addition, here are some great astrology sites:

www.astrologyzone.com: Susan Miller's site is a favorite for neophytes and pros alike. Every month she writes about several words per sign, with detailed predictions for the month. She cites the best days for romance, finances, and career matters. She discusses new and full moons, eclipses, and their impact on your sun sign, and provides information on various aspects that are coming up in a given month. You can also obtain a free natal chart. Her site is chocked with information and is user friendly, and her predictions are eerily accurate.

www.astro.com: This site is also jammed with information. Here you can get a free natal chart, see immediately where the planets are today, use the ephemeris, and find out the geographical coordinates for a particular city. There are other interesting tidbits as well—celebrities born on a given day and fascinating and informative articles by some of the world's best astrologers. This site is perfect for the beginner, the intermediary, and the advanced astrologer.

www.moonvalleyastrologer.com: Celeste Teal is *the* expert on eclipses, a specialized area of astrology that few have researched the way she has. Her two books on eclipses are seminal works. She also provides informative articles on various aspects of astrology. If you're new to astrology, there's plenty on this site to whet your appetite. Regardless of your expertise in astrology, Celeste's site offers information for everyone.

www.astrocollege.com: Lois Rodden's site is extraordinary. This woman spent most of her life collecting birth data and then created a piece of software that is invaluable in research. For example, you can compare charts of individuals in virtually any field and discover what astrological components they have in common. Let's say you're looking for artists who all had Leo suns, Capricorn moons, and Scorpio rising. You enter those criteria, and the software delivers names. The software also provides *signatures*—a certain combination of aspects and other factors that points to particular characteristics in an individual. In addition, the site rates and sells astrology software. Lois has passed on, but her work survives.

http://astrofuturetrends.com: Author and astrologer Anthony Louis does just what the site says. He predicts future trends, covers political stuff, and provides an overall view of astrology.

www.starlightnews.com: Click on *Nancy's blog*. Here you'll find the latest predictions and insights about world affairs. Nancy's predictions about politics have been right on. Before the 2004 election she made some predictions about tight senatorial races that were totally accurate. She also called the presidential race in 2008. Since we're writing this in early 2012, we don't know yet what her predictions are for 2012, but she'll undoubtedly prove to be accurate. She receives hundreds of comments for her posts, and some of them are as informative as her posts.

www.synchrosecrets.com/synchrosecrets: About synchronicities—what they are, how they show up in our lives, what they might mean, and hundreds of stories. There are occasional posts on astrological factors—like Mercury retrogrades!

Software

In the days before computers a natal chart or anything else connected to astrology had to be configured manually, through complicated mathematical formulae that left you gasping. Astrology software has truly transformed the study of astrology and our knowledge about it. Since the late 1980s, when we began using astrology software, the choices have multiplied.

Our first piece of software was a really simply program we found at a computer store for ten bucks. It erected a chart in about sixty seconds. There it was, rising, moon, sun, planets, the houses, everything set up on the computer screen as if by magic. In the late 1990s we bought our first really terrific astrology software from Matrix for about $300. In the years since, **http://www.astrologysoftware.com** has supplied us with endless data and information and revolutionized the study of astrology.

But it's not just enough to have a great piece of software. When your computer crashes, when you receive updates that screw up, when Windows updates to a new system, you call the Matrix help line and their people walk you through it until everything works. And the employees on their help lines aren't outsourced. You won't reach India. You'll talk to someone in Michigan who is not only an astrologer, but a computer geek who knows how to fix your problem. And if by some fluke they can't fix your problem, they'll credit you for one of their other terrific programs.

The only complaint we have about Matrix is that to activate the software, you have to call or contact them through the Internet to receive a special code. If your computer crashes, if you buy a new PC or laptop . . . well, it's annoying. When you pay this much for software, you shouldn't have to obtain a special access code.

Another great piece of software is SolarFire. Astrologers are as dedicated to this program as they are to Matrix's software. Check out http://www.alabe.com for current prices. While the two programs offer similar features and capabilities, preferences seem to be individual. Both Matrix's Winstar and astrolabe's SolarFire offer many of the same features—natal charts, transits, progressed charts, solar chart, and interpretations. They both feature material about fixed stars, aspects, lunations, eclipses, and all the other important components you could possibly want or need. The main difference lies in the appearance of the charts and how the information is presented.

Kepler's astrology program—http://www.astrosoftware.com—is beautiful in its rendition of charts, interpretations, and just about anything any astrologer could use or need. We like it for its ease, its beauty. But it lacks the complexity of both Winstar and Solar-Fire. The program simply doesn't do as much.

If your exploration of astrology takes you deeper, there are other software programs that take you there. Bernadette Brady is the undisputed mistress of fixed stars. Her software program, Starlight, is remarkable not only for its accuracy, but for its presentation. You will never think of fixed stars in the same way once you play with this program. What won't make sense in a natal chart interpretation suddenly snaps into clarity when you use her software. Be sure to download a print to file version for the software—through a PDF file—so that you can maximize usage. Their website: http://www.zyntara.com.

Lois Rodden's AstroDatabank is the software that Lois Rodden developed. It contains over thirty thousand birth records, "carefully documented and coded for accuracy with the popular Rodden Rating system. AstroDatabank includes intriguing biographies, revealing personality traits, important life events, and significant relationships." For the curious, the researcher, the neophyte and pro alike.

Both Winstar and SolarFire produce computerized report software. These reports are handy for when a friend of a friend is in a fix and you don't have the time to interpret transits and progressions for the person's birth chart. Winstar also produces software on other divination systems.

Day Watch, another Winstar program, is forecasting software that is invaluable for astrologers. From their site: "Certainly it creates personalized astrological calendars, a great tool for professional astrologers and those who have an understanding of astrological terms, symbols, and technique. But Day Watch also contains a full range of onscreen and printable interpretations of events that even someone with absolutely no astrological training can read, understand, and immediately put to use in their daily lives."

At the beginning of every month we bring up our personalized calendars that tell us what is happening daily in our natal charts and also lists which planets are changing signs in that month, on what date, and which planets are turning retrograde or direct. Each month includes an ephemeris and lunar charts for the new and full moon. The program also offers various types of reports.

Keep in mind that these programs are only for Windows. They don't work with the Mac operating system. As far as we know, there's just one program for Macs—the IO Edition, developed by Time Cycles Research. It lacks the bells and whistles of Winstar, but is certainly good enough for a natal chart and transits.

Getting a Reading

So now you're ready for an astrological reading. But where do you start? Which astrologer should you use?

The best way to find an astrologer is through someone who has gotten a reading and recommends the individual. If you don't know anyone who has had an astrological reading, the next best course is to head over to the nearest bookstore and look through the astrology books. Browse through titles that interest you. Note the author's style. If the author uses a lot of astro jargon or seems to write in a depressing or heavy-handed way, move on. Once you find an author whose book you like, check to see if he or she has a Web site. Most astrologers these days have Web sites that spell out their fees, what types of readings are offered, and a contact address.

Rates for a reading vary from one astrologer to another and usually depend on what you want. Would you like just an interpretation of your natal chart? Would you like a forecast for the next six months or a year? Do you want a compatibility chart for you and your partner? Some astrologers prefer to do phone readings and record the reading. Others prefer to work through e-mail. If the astrologer you've chosen lives close to you, all the better. Have the reading done in person.

What to Expect During a Reading

Every astrological reading begins with your natal chart, so an accurate birth time is essential. It should come from your birth certificate or a parent's memory. An approximate time means the entire reading won't be as accurate. Over the years we've done way too many readings that turned out to be based on inaccurate birth times and then had to construct an accurate chart. If you don't know your time of birth, it's possible to rectify your chart based on major events in your life—the date of your marriage or divorce, a major move, the death of a parent. But this process is time consuming and rarely as accurate as an exact birth time.

A reading with an astrologer differs from a daily horoscope you find in a newspaper or even on a Web site. It's tailored to your specific chart rather than just to your sun sign. If you're getting a reading only on your birth chart, the astrologer interprets the entire chart, not just pieces of it. The astrologer looks at the signs and house placements of the various planets and the angles the planets make to each other.

If you want predictions for the next six or twelve months, the astrologer uses various techniques that are all based on your natal chart. Transits—the daily motion of the planets—have the most immediate impact on our lives, so the astrologer will first look at how the slower-moving planets—Pluto, Neptune, Uranus—impact your chart. Since they stay in the same sign for the greatest length of time, their influence can be felt for decades. The transits of both Saturn and Jupiter are taken into account too.

Usually the astrologer will pay close attention to how the transits of your chart's ruler are affecting you. If you have Scorpio rising, the transits of Pluto and Mars (the coruler) would be important. If you have Gemini rising, Mercury's transits would be important. The astrologer should also consider how eclipses and the new and full moons might affect you, particularly when there's a lunation in the same sign as your natal sun, moon, or rising.

Another predictive technique the astrologer should use is one called progression. In this technique your natal chart is progressed forward in time to the present. Since the moon is the swiftest-moving planet, moving about one progressed degree a month, the progressed chart provides timing. An astrologer can time events down to a month.

Yet another predictive technique is called the solar return chart, where your sun sign is returned to where it was at your birth. This chart's influence extends from one birthday to the next and when compared with the natal chart provides additional information and insights about what you can expect during the next twelve months.

An astrologer may also take a look at other elements in your chart, or if you have a specific question can erect an horary chart for that particular question. Horary and medical astrology are specialized fields and not all astrologers are competent to answer questions using this technique.

CHAPTER 13

By the Numbers

Even though this is an astrology book, we use numbers in some of the daily predictions because we're attempting to remain true to what Sydney Omarr did. The legendary astrologer was also a numerologist and combined the two forms in his work. So let's take a closer look at how the numbers work.

If you're familiar with numerology, you probably know your life path number, which is derived from your birth date. That number represents who you were at birth and the traits that you'll carry throughout your life. There are numerous books and Web sites that provide details on what the numbers mean regarding your life path.

But in the daily predictions, what does it mean when it's a number 9 day, and how did it get to be that number? In the dailies you'll usually find these numbers on the days when the moon is transiting from one sign to another. The system is simple: add the numbers related to the astrological sign (1 for Aries, 2 for Taurus, etc.), the year, the month, and the day.

For example, to find what number June 14, 2014, is

for a Libra, you would start with 7, the number for Libra, add 7 (the number you get when you add 2014 together), plus 6 for June, plus 5 (1+4) for the day. That would be 7+7+6+5 (sign + year + month+ day) = 25 or 7. So June 14, 2014, is a number 7 day for a Libra. It would be an 8 day for a Scorpio, the sign following Libra. So on that number 7 day Libra might be advised that his investigative and research skills are especially strong, and he should explore his spiritual beliefs and venture into the unknown.

Briefly here are the meanings of the numbers, which are included in more detail in the dailies themselves.

1) Taking the lead, getting a fresh start, a new beginning
2) Cooperation, partnership, a new relationship, sensitivity
3) Harmony, beauty, pleasures of life, warm, receptive
4) Getting organized, hard work, being methodical, rebuilding, fulfilling your obligations
5) Freedom of thought and action, change, variety, thinking outside the box
6) A service day, being diplomatic, generous, tolerant, sympathetic
7) Mystery, secrets, investigations, research, detecting deception, exploration of the unknown, of the spiritual realms
8) Your power day, financial success, unexpected money, a windfall
9) Finishing a project, looking beyond the immediate, setting your goals, reflection, expansion.

Simple, right?

Once you become accustomed to what the numbers mean for a particular day, you can adjust your attitude and thoughts accordingly. After all, how a day, week, month, or year unfolds depends more on your attitude toward yourself and your world than it does on any number or astrology sign. If you practice waking up each morning in a spirit of adventure and gratitude, pretty soon it becomes second nature, and your life shifts accordingly. Sound like magical thinking? It is. Try it, and watch your life change.

CHAPTER 14

Matters of the Heart for Cancer in 2014

Love and romance: don't most of us hope for the perfect relationship? For a soul mate? Astrology is the perfect tool for alerting us to periods when everything is working in our favor—or not—in the arena of love. If we're going to come up against challenges, what are those challenges likely to be and how can we prepare for them? If we're entering a period when love is in the air, how can we maximize the energies?

In this area we look at the transits of Venus as well as the angles Venus is making to your sun sign. If you know, for instance, when Venus is making a difficult angle to your sun sign, you can expect challenges in your love life. If you know when Venus is going to be in your sun sign, you can expect a harmonious period.

There are other factors, of course, that have a bearing on your love life. What is Mars doing at any given time? As the planet that symbolizes your sexuality, aggression, and ambition, its transits and the angles it makes to Venus and to your sun sign are important. Then there are lunar transits. The moon—symbolic of your emotions, inner life, ability to nurture, and intuition—is also important. You can see how this could get complicated very quickly. So let's keep things simple and take a look at just the Venus transits in 2014. We'll pinpoint time periods for you that are both propitious and challenging for love and romance and for your creative endeavors.

Venus Transits in 2014 That Make Your Heart Sing

The two best periods this year occur between **July 18 and August 12,** when Venus transits your sign, and between **October 23 and November 16,** when Venus moves through Scorpio and your solar fifth house.

During this first period you exude great sex appeal and charm, and everyone is clamoring for your attention. You're very in synch with who you are, your self-confidence rises, and these feelings in turn attract new relationship opportunities. Your muse is also extremely cooperative during this transit. She's whispering in your ear as you dream, at your beck and call when you're awake. Creativity is your middle name during this transit, so don't waste the opportunity.

The second period is sure to be enjoyable. If you get involved in a relationship during this transit, it's strictly for fun and pleasure. Although it may develop into something later on, you're not concerned about anything deeper right now. If you're already in a committed relationship, then this transit spells all the enjoyment that brought the two of you together to begin with.

Your creative drive during this transit is especially

strong. You're very intense, looking for the bottom line in any creative endeavor. You're also intent on doing things you enjoy and hanging out with people who make you feel good about yourself and the world in general, i.e., optimistic, upbeat people. Synchronicity could be frequent during this transit, so pay close attention to the sign posts the universe posts along the way.

During each of these transits your water-sign qualities are enhanced and strengthened. If you're a nurturing, intuitive Cancer, then you become more so. If you're a clingy Cancer, one who has to control everything around you, then you also become more so. For many Cancers home is your castle, and that castle could be anything—a house, apartment, condo, even a camper. You may decide to move during this transit or beautify your home in some way. You and your partner may undertake a beautification of your home together.

Good Backups

April 5–May 2: Venus transits fellow water sign Pisces, your solar ninth house. This transit favors romance while traveling, in an educational setting, or even while pursuing spiritual studies. Pisces is an intuitive, imaginative sign, so you may be attracted to individuals who have these qualities.

September 5–29: Venus transits compatible earth sign Virgo, your solar third house. This transit is fun for you, whether you're involved or not. Your mood is lighter, you're more social, you're eager to get out and be seen. You could meet someone special through siblings, friends, or neighbors. You may be somewhat finicky, however, following a mental checklist of what you want—and don't want—in a relationship.

In a romantic relationship you and your partner may be more open to communicating what you feel about each other and about the relationship generally.

May 28–June 23: Venus transits compatible earth sign Taurus, your solar eleventh house. This one could bring someone interesting into your life through social networks or friends. Your imagination and ability to visualize what you want are quite strong during this period. Any relationship that begins during this transit will be sensuous and grounded.

January 1–March 5 and December 10–January 4, 2015: Venus transits Capricorn, your opposite sign. Opposites attract!

Challenging Transits

May 2–28: Venus transits fire sign Aries. Unless you have a lot of fire-sign planets in your natal chart, this transit may irritate you. You may feel edgy and restless and think that a partner is trying to dominate you or is being too possessive.

June 23–July 18: Venus transits air sign Gemini, your solar twelfth house. Unless you have a lot of air signs in your natal chart, this won't be your favorite transit. Hidden stuff in a relationship may surface. There may be a lot of communication drama during this period. You may be short-tempered. People around you seem to be pressing your buttons!

August 12–September 5: Venus transits fire sign

Leo. Many Cancers shy away from the limelight. If you're like that, then this transit could be challenging. You may be pushed into the limelight for some reason and have to become someone you aren't.

November 16–December 10: Venus moves through fire sign Sagittarius, your solar sixth house. You may be distracted by a flirtation or full-blown affair in which you become involved with an employee or co-worker.

When Love Is Intuitive

As a water sign, your approach to love and romance is usually intuitive. If the person feels right to you, then you get involved. If your intuitive compass says there's something off about the person, you run in the opposite direction. There are two periods when your intuitive compass will be exceptionally powerful:

May 28–June 23: Venus transits earth sign Taurus. Taurus is usually regarded as a grounded yet sensuous sign. But Taurus can also be quite mystical and psychic, and your intuitive compass should be working flawlessly.

October 23–November 16: Venus transits Scorpio. As we said earlier, this period is one of the most romantic and creative for you all year, but it's also an intuitive transit. Scorpio strengthens your natural abilities, and it's unlikely that anyone can put over anything on you.

In the next chapter we'll take a look at what Mars is doing this year and how its transits could impact your sexuality.

CHAPTER 15

Your Sexuality and Ambition in 2014

In astrology Mars rules your sexuality, physical energy, ambition, and drive and can sometimes have an indirect effect on your health. In this chapter we're going to take a look at how the Mars transits in 2014 affect these areas—and inadvertently your love life!

A positive angle between Mars and your sun sign often acts as a booster rocket; you have more physical energy, drive, and ambition. A challenging angle can be just plain frustrating. Either way, though, if you're informed about when positive and challenging angles are approaching and how to deal with them, then you're empowered.

For the first two months of the year Mars is moving in direct motion in air sign Libra, your solar fourth house, your domestic environment. During this period you may be doing a lot of stuff in and around your home—repairing, expanding, painting, cleaning out closets. You may also be working out of your home for some reason. Since Mars is in Libra, there's a social element to this transit. You may be hosting a few dinner parties at your place and are involved more in social media networking, perhaps to advertise your or your company's service or products.

If you're involved in a committed relationship, you and your partner may be spending more time at home. If you're not involved, you could meet someone special through friends or a family member, and the sexual chemistry is good.

Between March 1 and May 19 Mars ceases to function at optimum levels because it moves retrograde. During this period you may revisit sexuality issues you thought were solved, or your sex life may not be as vigorous as you hoped. Also, social relationships and your team efforts may not go as planned. Something is *off*.

It's easy to feel frustrated when Mars is moving retrograde, and the best way to deal with it is to go the extra mile in everything you do. On the creative front, work extra hours on your projects, but only if you enjoy doing so. Forget working on major repairs or expansions to your home during the retro period, unless you absolutely have to. It's important with this retrograde—and the entire transit—to stick to what you enjoy, what you feel passionate about.

While Mars is in Libra, retrograde or in direct motion, try to see things from your partner's point of view. Be more cooperative than you usually are. Rather than resist, try to go with the flow, whatever it is.

Between May 19 and July 25, with Mars in direct motion again, the texture of things is similar to what it was before the retrograde began.

From July 27 to September 13 Mars transits fellow water sign Scorpio, a sign it corules and your solar fifth house. You aggressively pursue love, romance, creative endeavors, and anything and everything you enjoy. Your sexuality is certainly heightened too. Since Mars is now forming a beneficial angle to your sun sign, your intuitive abilities are strengthened, and there's an intuitive component to your sexuality and ambition. It's as if you're *feeling* your way forward through these various areas.

Mars in Scorpio is a sexually charged transit. If you're involved with someone, your relationship goes through an intense sexual period. If you get involved during this transit, the relationship may be based on sexual chemistry.

The period from September 13 to October 26 may bring on a need to travel, to break away from your routine. Mars transits fire sign Sagittarius, your solar sixth house, so there's a lot of emphasis on the maintenance of your health and daily work routine. But it's the Sadge component that brings on the restlessness, the need to travel, to exert your independence. So it's likely that this transit will be one of contradictions. Obligation versus desire.

Between October 26 and December 4 Mars transits Capricorn, your opposite sign. This transit places emphasis on both your business and personal relationships. If you're in a relationship, you and your partner may deepen your commitment to each other—you get engaged, married, move in together. Regardless of your relationship status, you may feel more ambitious during this period—that's the Capricorn!—and will need to balance the various components of your life.

Then we arrive at the Mars transit through Aquarius, between December 4 and January 12, 2015. This transit occurs in your solar eighth house. Your partner's income may come under your spotlight. You aggressively pursue additional income, or you may volunteer your time on a worthy project. If you're in the midst of a divorce, the question of resources could be a bone of contention. Aquarius sets trends, leads rather than follows, so you may meet unusual and idiosyncratic people who spark your sexual and romantic interest.

Other Important Dates

On June 27 there's a new moon in your sign, Saturn is in fellow water sign Scorpio, and Neptune is in fellow water sign Pisces. These elements add up to new opportunities that somehow involve your idealism and spiritual beliefs and greater structure and responsibility. Sounds like a job promotion, a raise, a chance to really flex your creativity, Cancer.

January 15 features a full moon in your sign, with Jupiter widely conjunct. This one should be quite nice for you. Whatever culminates around the time of this full moon expands your life in some significant way. You may feel sort of nutty, but it's a loveable kind of nutty. Friends and family love you exactly as you are.

Keep a Record

In the space below keep a brief record of how each of these transits impacts your life. Over time you may recognize patterns emerging with certain transits of

Mars. With access to the Internet, you can also check on how combined transits impact your life.

Let's say that while Mars is moving through fellow water sign Scorpio, a new love relationship begins or a creative project is offered to you. Note the time and date and then use the Internet to find out what the other planets were doing when this opportunity came along. You may discover that the moon was in your sign or another water sign or even a fire sign.

The purpose of this record is to grasp the patterns to which you're sensitive. If you don't already have a copy of your natal chart, by all means get one. Web sites that offer free natal charts are listed elsewhere in the book. The more information you have, the better prepared you'll be to take advantage of beneficial transits before they arrive!

_____

_____

_____

_____

_____

_____

_____

_____

_____

_____

_____

_____

_____

_____

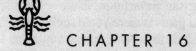

CHAPTER 16

Career Timing for Cancer in 2014

Your tenth house symbolizes your career, your public persona. Transits through this house can reveal a lot about your professional life—opportunities that may surface, challenges that may arise. Also, certain transits through your sun sign are important too in terms of professional matters. Now let's take a closer look at what's emerging in your career in 2014.

One of the best dates this year for professional matters falls on March 30, with a new moon in your career area. Uranus forms a close conjunction with this new moon, suggesting that opportunities occur suddenly, without warning. This mean you've got to be on your toes, Cancer, ready to seize the opportunities as they arrive. This one could bring a new job, new career path, promotion, raise, new boss. You may take greater risks now, and the potential payoff could be significant.

One of the best dates for you in terms of your career and just about everything else occurs on June 27, with a new moon in your sign, Cancer. This moon happens just once a year and sets the tone of things for the next twelve months, so it's wise to prepare for it. About a week before the new moon, make a list of professional goals and post it where you'll see it often. Back these goals and desires with strong emotion. Then on the day of the new moon, release them by tossing out the list. Now move aside and let the universe manifest these desires.

Jupiter is also in your sign at this time, so these new opportunities are about expansion. If you've been looking for employment, this new moon could help you find the right job at the right time. Thanks to a beneficial angle from Neptune, these leads could come through a church group or a charity for which you volunteer. If you've applied for college or graduate school, you could hear the news that you've been accepted around the time of this new moon.

Between May 2 and 28 Venus transits Aries, your solar tenth house. During this period your life may feel like it's jammed in fast forward. You're a trailblazer, the one who takes risks that pay off, the one whose ideas are cutting edge. Bosses and peers look to you for guidance and leadership. Use your considerable intuition during this period, Cancer. It won't steer you wrong.

Venus in Aries is driven by strong passions, independence, restlessness, and impatience. You may feel that only you can do a particular job the right way and end up burning out. Launch your ideas, projects, creative endeavors, then delegate!

Until July 16 expansive Jupiter is in your sign, so you'll have the Midas touch! This transit acts as a kind of protection too, as long as you don't overextend yourself.

Between April 7 and 23 Mercury transits your career sector. This period is great for pitching ideas, submitting manuscripts, brainstorming with coworkers, family, friends, whoever wants to be involved. Be sure to keep extensive notes. Also, with Mercury in Aries, you think very far outside the box, so don't hesitate to express your ideas. You may want to start a blog or Web site on your or your company's services and products.

Other good periods fall between May 29 and June 17 and July 12 and 31, when Mercury is moving direct in your sign. During these transits you're exceptionally intuitive. Your conscious mind is like a sponge, absorbing the feelings and moods of people around you. You're able to tune in on people, read them accurately, and know exactly what to say and when to say it.

In between these dates Mercury is retrograde in your sign. Try to plan meetings and launch ideas and projects on either side of the retrograde.

This year Mars doesn't transit your career area. However, when Mars transits fire sign Sagittarius, it forms a beneficial angle to your career area. This occurs between September 13 and October 26. You may travel for business, and that trip could turn into some sort of spiritual quest. Mars in Sadge enables you to grasp the larger picture of your professional life and daily work. Use these insights; take them to heart.

Between July 16 and August 11, 2015, Jupiter transits Leo and your financial area and forms a strong, beneficial angle to your solar tenth house. Possibilities? A better-paying job, a substantial raise, you sell a novel or book, receive an insurance settlement, find a new career that's more in line with your deeper beliefs. Expansion, expansion!

Jupiter's transit through Leo enables you to exhibit your many talents and skills in a way that others applaud. You receive the recognition you deserve.

If you're unemployed this is the ideal time to send out résumés and schedule interviews. Prospective employers will be attracted to your ideas and to you personally. You come off as smart, savvy, charming, reliable.

If you work in the arts, the period between October 23 and November 16 is perfect. Venus transits Scorpio, your solar fifth house of creativity. Your muse is ready for intensive work, and the transit enables you to dig deeply into yourself to produce extraordinary work. This period is one of the most creative all year, so put it to use, Cancer.

The other transit we should mention involves Saturn. Without this planet our lives would lack structure and discipline, and the universe and everything in it would be complete chaos. Between July 20 and December 23 Saturn is moving direct, through Scorpio, and forming a beneficial angle to your sun. This transit, which has been going on since October 2012, provides exactly the right structure for your creativity. Your research and investigative skills are heightened and so is your intuition. Inspiration and ideas may come to you through dreams, while meditating, or even when you're simply relaxing. You have a clearer understanding of the bottom line in whatever you tackle professionally and are able to connect all the dots on a daily basis in your work.

This transit of Saturn suggests that you may be assuming more responsibility for your own creativity, services, and products. Sounds like you could be going into business for yourself, Cancer!

On December 23 Saturn enters Sagittarius, your solar sixth house. This transit lasts for two and a half years and forms a dynamic angle to your career area. Foreign travel, publishing, and higher education are highlighted. If you're looking for employment when this transit begins, it should help you land the right job!

CHAPTER 17

The Big Picture for Cancer in 2014

Welcome to 2014, Cancer! It's a 2 year for you, which emphasizes partnerships, cooperation, teamwork. It's a year when it's easier for two people joined together to achieve something than it is for two separate individuals to accomplish the same thing. Now that the tumult of 2012 and the realignment of 2013 are behind you, you're ready to embark on yet another journey.

So let's look at how specific areas of your life may be impacted and which dates will be of vital importance to you.

Romance/Creativity

One of the most romantic and creative times for you all year occurs between July 18 and August 12, when Venus transits your sign. During this period your muse is at your beck and call, and you feel so creative that everything you touch illustrates how your muse is working for you. You feel more self-confident, and others pick up on that vibe and are attracted to you, your ideas, your persona, your creative projects. So if you have creative products ready, start submitting and exhibiting them, doing whatever you need to do in order to advertise your products.

If a relationship begins during this period, it's likely to be deeply intuitive. You and your partner will have similar interests and a solid base for communication. The romantic interests you attract are a reflection of who you are within the most profound depths of your soul. If you're already involved in a relationship, this transit helps to define it. You and your partner may deepen your commitment to each other.

The other terrific period for romance and creativity occurs between October 23 and November 16, when Venus transits fellow water sign Scorpio, your solar fifth house. This transit stimulates you to do whatever it is you most enjoy. Many Scorpios enjoy exploring metaphysics, so you may undertake a spiritual quest of some kind. Or you may be doing extensive research into something. It's a perfect time for romance, the romantic kind of romance that entails long talks, candlelit dinners, concerts, exchanging ideas, browsing bookstore aisles together, doing the sorts of things so many Cancers enjoy.

Between January 1 and July 16 Jupiter moves through your sign, a continuation of a transit that began last year. Jupiter expands whatever it touches, so this entire transit should be magnificent for you in all areas. Between July 16 and August 11, 2015, Jupiter moves through Leo and your financial area, so this period should improve your monetary situation! When you feel secure financially, other areas of your life tend to flow more easily.

Other excellent dates:

April 5–May 2, Venus in fellow water sign Pisces forms a beautiful angle to your sun and Jupiter. Heightened intuition in all areas of your life. Romance may find you while you're traveling or while you're involved in creative work.

October 23, a new moon in Scorpio, your solar fifth house. This one should bring new romantic possibilities and a chance to do something new creatively. You may also uncover new enjoyments and pleasures.

Be sure to consult the chapter Matters of the Heart for more details on good dates for romance and creative ventures.

Career

Jupiter's transit through Leo will help every facet of your life, even your career. The caveat with career matters, though, is that if you're doing something you love, you benefit tremendously. If you're working in a field that doesn't excite you, that has become rather humdrum and routine, then Jupiter, Mars, Venus, Mercury, and your ruler, the moon, could help you to break away and find something that is more aligned with your passions. Be sure to check at one of the online sites suggested earlier in the book to find out when the moon is in your sign each month.

Let's take a closer look at the beneficial career times:

April 7–23: Mercury is moving direct in Aries, through your career area. This period favors communication with bosses and peers. This is the time to pitch your ideas, move professional matters forward. Start a blog, put up a Web site, advertise your products/services or those of your company. Your conscious mind is quite free-spirited and independent.

May 2–28: During this period while Venus transits your career area, your professional life is exciting, perhaps even somewhat feverish. This time frame is perfect for pushing your own ideas and beliefs forward in your work. Coworkers and bosses are impressed with your ideas and the way you implement them.

March 30: The new moon in Aries, your career area, should usher in new professional opportunities. Uranus forms a close conjunction with this new moon, suggesting an unexpected quality to any opportunities that surface.

Between September 13 and October 26 Mars in Sagittarius forms a beneficial angle to your career area. This transit may bring foreign travel connected to professional matters. Your desire for independence is strong. Maybe this is the time to launch your own business?

Finances

Let's look at the Jupiter transit first for beneficial dates for finances. Your solar second house, which rules money, is in Leo, so the entire thirteen months that Jupiter is in Leo should be terrific for your monetary situation. Those dates: July 16, 2014, to August 11, 2015. You could see a significant rise in your income. You could get a raise or royalty check, your partner could land a raise, money could come through an insurance settlement. Regardless of the source, this transit benefits your finances.

Other good dates? August 12–September 5, when Venus is in Leo, your financial area.

July 26 features a new moon in Leo, which could attract new financial opportunities and sources of income.

Mercury Retrogrades

Every year Mercury—the planet of communication and travel—turns retrograde three times. During these periods it's wise not to sign contracts (unless you don't mind renegotiating when Mercury is moving direct), to check and recheck travel plans, and to communicate as succinctly as possible. Refrain from buying any large-ticket items or electronics during this time too. Often computers and appliances go on the fritz, cars act up, data is lost . . . you get the idea. Be sure to back up all files before the dates below:

February 6–28: Mercury retrograde in Pisces, your solar ninth house. This one impacts foreign travel. Mercury slips back into Aquarius before it turns direct, so it impacts your joint resources too. Be sure to check and recheck bank statements.

June 7–July 1: Mercury retrograde in your sign. This retrograde may make you feel as if your personal life is in chaos. It really isn't, but the retrograde makes it impossible to ignore issues you should tackle and resolve.

October 4–25: Mercury retrograde in Scorpio, your

solar fifth house. This one impacts your love life and creative work. Be sure to communicate succinctly and clearly with everyone in your work environment—employees, coworkers, bosses. If you receive a worrisome health report, get rechecked after Mercury turns direct again.

Eclipses

Solar eclipses tend to trigger external events that bring about change according to the sign and house in which they fall. Lunar eclipses trigger inner, emotional events according to the sign and house in which they fall. Any eclipse marks both beginnings and endings. The solar and lunar eclipse in a pair falls in opposite signs. If you're interested in detailed information on eclipses, take a look at Celeste Teal's excellent and definitive book, *Eclipses: Predicting World Events & Personal Transformation*.

If you were born under or around the time of an eclipse, it's to your advantage to take a look at your birth chart to find out exactly where the eclipses will impact you.

Most years feature four eclipses—two solar, two lunar—with the set separated by about two weeks. Let's take a closer look.

April 15: Lunar eclipse in Libra, your solar fourth house. Emotional issues surface related to your domestic situation. The emotions are positive, though!

April 29: Solar eclipse in Taurus, your solar eleventh house. New opportunities for working with groups and friends and networking. It's a good time to join a gym or sign up for yoga classes. With Mercury forming a close conjunction to the eclipse degree, Jupiter forming a beneficial angle to it, and both Mercury and Jupiter forming great angles to your sun sign, the opportunities will be expansive.

October 8: Lunar eclipse in Aries, your solar tenth house. Uranus is closely conjunct the moon, so you can expect sudden and unexpected emotional issues related to your career and professional life.

October 23: Solar eclipse in Scorpio, your solar fifth house. New romantic possibilities and opportunities to show off your creative abilities.

The Luckiest Days of 2014

Every year there are one or two days when Jupiter and the sun meet up, and luck, serendipity, and expansion are the hallmarks. This year those days fall on July 25–26. Circle the dates. Do whatever you enjoy!

CHAPTER 18

Eighteen Months of Day-by-Day Predictions: July 2013 to December 2014

Moon sign times are calculated for Eastern Standard Time and Eastern Daylight Time. Please adjust for your local time zone.

JULY 2013

Monday, July 1 (Moon into Taurus, 4:44 p.m.)   It's a number 9 day, your day to finish up what you've been working on and get ready for something new. Take time to reflect on what you've been doing, and look for a way to expand. Visualize the future; set your goals, then make them so.

Tuesday, July 2 (Moon in Taurus)   The moon is in your eleventh house today. You get along better with friends and associates. Your sense of security is tied to your relationships. Work for the common good, but keep an eye on your own wishes and dreams.

Wednesday, July 3 (Moon in Taurus)   Health and physical activity are highlighted. It's a good time for gardening, cultivating ideas, doing practical things. While you maintain a common-sense, down-to-earth perspective on life, you also long for the good life with its material blessings.

Thursday, July 4 (Moon into Gemini, 4:23 a.m.) Your imagination is keen now, and you communicate well. You're curious and inventive. You're warm and receptive to what others say. Enjoy the harmony, beauty, and pleasures of life. You have a strong sense of duty and feel obligated to fulfill your promises.

Friday, July 5 (Moon in Gemini) The moon is in your twelfth house today. You might feel a need to withdraw and work on your own. Think carefully before you act. There's a tendency now to undo all the positive actions you've taken. Avoid any self-destructive behavior. Be aware of hidden enemies.

Saturday, July 6 (Moon into Cancer, 5:14 p.m.) It's a number 2 day. That means partnerships and co-operation are highlighted. Help comes through friends or loved ones, especially a partner. Don't make waves. Don't rush or show resentment; let things develop. You could be undergoing some soul-searching related to a relationship now.

Sunday, July 7 (Moon in Cancer) Saturn goes direct in your fifth house today. Issues related to a creative project or to children in your life are resolved. Also, difficulties related to a romance or relationship are over. You need to enhance the base or foundation of a creative project or relationship.

Monday, July 8 (Moon in Cancer) There's a new moon in your first house today, and four other planets are also in Cancer! That means the focus is on your personal life, your health and emotions. You're dealing with the person you are becoming. New opportunities come your way now. You're feeling recharged and ready to go. You're physically vital, and relations with the opposite sex go well.

Tuesday, July 9 (Moon into Leo, 5:48 a.m.) It's a number 8 day, your power day. Business discussions go well. You attract financial success. Open your mind to a new approach that could bring in big bucks. You have a chance to expand, to gain recognition, even fame and power.

Wednesday, July 10 (Moon in Leo) The moon is in your second house today. You tend to react emotionally now to an event in your life related to money or your values. You identify emotionally with your possessions or whatever you value. Look at your priorities in handling your income. Watch your spending.

Thursday, July 11 (Moon into Virgo, 5:12 p.m.) It's a number 1 day, and you're at the top of your cycle. You take the lead in something new and get a fresh start, a new beginning. Stress originality. You attract creative people now and avoid those with closed minds. Trust your hunches.

Friday, July 12 (Moon in Virgo) The moon is in your third house today. You write from a deep place today; it's a good day for journaling. Be aware that your thinking may be unduly influenced by things from the past. You could be visiting with relatives or siblings or spending time in the community with your neighbors. You accept an invitation to a social event.

Saturday, July 13 (Moon in Virgo)   With Mars moving into your first house today, you're quite outgoing and assertive now, letting others know exactly what you think and how you feel. Others see you as ambitious. Your feelings and thoughts are aligned.

Sunday, July 14 (Moon into Libra, 2:41 a.m.)   It's a number 4 day. Tear down the old in order to rebuild. Be methodical and thorough. Take care of your obligations. Your organizational skills are highlighted. You tend to stay with the tried and true. It's not a day for experimentation or new approaches.

Monday, July 15 (Moon in Libra)   The moon is in your fourth house. You're dealing with the foundations of who you are and who you are becoming. Retreat to a private place for meditation. It's a good day for dream recall. Change a bad habit. A parent plays a role.

Tuesday, July 16 (Moon into Scorpio, 9:25 a.m.) It's a number 6 day, a service day. Adjust to the needs of loved ones. Diplomacy wins the day. Focus on making people happy. Be sympathetic, kind, and compassionate. You serve, teach, and guide. But know when to say enough is enough.

Wednesday, July 17 (Moon in Scorpio)   Uranus goes retrograde in your tenth house today and stays that way until December 17. That means you might be doing some soul-searching about your career goals. You could be getting flashes of inspiration related to what you really want to do. Matters are somewhat unpredictable over the next few months. Avoid going to extremes. Pushing yourself too hard could result in accidents. Watch your step! Be careful when talking on your cell and driving, Cancer.

Thursday, July 18 (Moon into Sagittarius, 12:55 p.m.) It's your power day, Cancer, and your day to play it your way. Think big and act big! You can go far with your plans and achieve financial success, especially if you open your mind to a new approach.

Friday, July 19 (Moon in Sagittarius) The moon is in your sixth house today, Cancer. People look to you for help. You can improve whatever others are working on. Keep your resolutions about exercise, and watch your diet. Attend to details related to your health. Make a doctor or dentist appointment.

Saturday, July 20 (Moon into Capricorn, 1:40 p.m.) Mercury goes direct in your first house today. That means any confusion, miscommunication, and delays that you've been experiencing, especially related to a health or personal matter, recede into the past. Things move more smoothly now. You get your ideas across.

Sunday, July 21 (Moon in Capricorn) The moon is in your seventh house today. You get along well with others now. You can fit in just about anywhere. Loved ones and partners are more important than usual. Take time to consider how others see you. You're in the public eye.

Monday, July 22 (Moon into Aquarius, 1:08 p.m.)
Venus moves into your third house today, and that means you get along well with your family, because you don't want to argue. You're also more willing to compromise over the next three weeks. With the full moon in your eighth house, you have a better understanding of matters such as a mortgage, taxes, credit cards, or insurance. You could also gain insight related to a metaphysical subject such as astrology, ghosts, or past lives.

Tuesday, July 23 (Moon in Aquarius)   The moon is in your eighth house of shared resources and investments today. Your experiences are more intense than usual. You have a strong sense of duty and feel obligated to fulfill your promises. Security is an important issue with you right now. As yesterday, it's a good day for dealing with mortgages, insurance, and investments.

Wednesday, July 24 (Moon into Pisces, 1:23 p.m.)
It's a number 5 day. You're versatile and changeable now, but be careful not to spread yourself too thin. Release old structures; get a new point of view. Take a risk; experiment. Approach the day with an unconventional mindset.

Thursday, July 25 (Moon in Pisces)   The moon is in your ninth house today. Your mind is active, and you yearn for new experiences, a break from the routine, a change from the status quo. You can create positive change through your ideas now. A publishing project takes off. Publicity and advertising are emphasized.

Friday, July 26 (Moon into Aries, 4:30 p.m.)   It's your mystery day, Cancer. You could be dealing with confidential information and intrigue. Dig deep for information. Express your desires, but avoid self-deception. Make sure that you see things as they are, not as you wish them to be.

Saturday, July 27 (Moon in Aries)   The moon is in your tenth house today. Business dealings are highlighted on this Saturday. It's a good day for sales and dealing with the public. You get along well with fellow workers. Avoid any emotional displays in public.

Sunday, July 28 (Moon into Taurus, 11:44 p.m.) Finish what you started. Visualize the future; set your goals, then make them so. Look beyond the immediate. Get ready for something new, but don't start anything until tomorrow. Strive for universal appeal.

Monday, July 29 (Moon in Taurus)   The moon is in your eleventh house today. You get along better with friends and associates, who play an important role in your day. Focus on your wishes and dreams. Examine your overall goals. Those goals should be an expression of who you are. You get a fresh start.

Tuesday, July 30 (Moon in Taurus)   Health and physical activity are highlighted. It's a good time for gardening, cultivating ideas, doing practical things.

Use common sense, and take a down-to-earth perspective on whatever you're doing.

Wednesday, July 31 (Moon into Gemini, 10:42 a.m.)
Play your hunches now. Have fun today in preparation for tomorrow's discipline and focus. Make time to listen to others. You can influence people with your upbeat attitude. Take time to relax, enjoy yourself, recharge your batteries.

AUGUST 2013

Thursday, August 1 (Moon in Gemini)   The moon is in your twelfth house today. It's a good day to withdraw from the action and keep to yourself. Work on a solo project. Keep your feelings secret. Be aware that relations with women can be difficult now. Things affecting you from the past could surface.

Friday, August 2 (Moon into Cancer, 11:30 p.m.)   It's a number 2 day. Don't make waves. Don't rush or show resentment; let things develop. Cooperation is highlighted. Use your intuition to get a sense of your day.

Saturday, August 3 (Moon in Cancer)   The moon is on your ascendant today. That means the way you see yourself now is the way others see you. You're recharged for the month ahead, and this makes you more appealing to the public. You're physically vital, and you can expect relations with the opposite sex to go well.

Sunday, August 4 (Moon in Cancer)   The moon is in your first house today. You're dealing with the person you're becoming. Your self-awareness and appearance take on new meaning. It's all about your emotional self and your health. Your moods can shift from ebullient to sad and then back again in a short time.

Monday, August 5 (Moon into Leo, 11:58 a.m.) Get ready for change. It's a good day to experiment and let go of old structures. Variety is the spice of life. Release old structures. Promote new ideas, and follow your curiosity. Freedom of thought and action is key.

Tuesday, August 6 (Moon in Leo) The new moon is in your second house today, Cancer, and that means opportunities come your way related to money-making ideas. Financial matters work to your advantage now. With Uranus trine to the moon, you could be in for some pleasant surprises.

Wednesday, August 7 (Moon into Virgo, 10:58 p.m.) You take a journey into the unknown today. You could be dealing with confidential information and intrigue. Dig deep for information. Express your desires, but avoid self-deception. Make sure that you see things as they are, not as you wish them to be.

Thursday, August 8 (Moon in Virgo) Mercury moves into your second house. There's lots of mental stimulation now regarding finances. You communicate your fresh ideas related to money-making projects. You also discuss your insights into your values or whatever you value.

Friday, August 9 (Moon in Virgo)   The moon is in your third house today. Get your ideas across as you go about your everyday activities. Take what you've learned recently, and tell others about it. But avoid getting overly emotional, especially when dealing with neighbors or relatives.

Saturday, August 10 (Moon into Libra, 8:09 a.m.) You're at the top of your cycle again, Cancer. Trust your hunches today. You get a fresh start, a new beginning. You're inventive and make connections that others overlook. Don't be afraid to turn in a new direction.

Sunday, August 11 (Moon in Libra)   The moon is in your fourth house today. Spend time with your family and loved ones. Stick close to home, if possible. You could be dealing with parents now. You're dealing with the foundations of who you are and who you are becoming.

Monday, August 12 (Moon into Scorpio, 3:19 p.m.) Your attitude determines everything today. Ease up on routines, and spread your good news. You communicate well. You're warm and receptive to what others say. Remain flexible, and enjoy the harmony, beauty, and pleasures of life.

Tuesday, August 13 (Moon in Scorpio)   Romance and sex for pleasure are highlighted. Your emotions tend to overpower your intellect now, and you're in touch with your creative side. You feel strongly attached to loved ones, particularly children.

Wednesday, August 14 (Moon into Sagittarius, 8:05 p.m.)   It's a number 5 day. Freedom of thought and action is highlighted. Change your perspective. Approach the day with an unconventional mindset. Promote new ideas; follow your curiosity. You can overcome obstacles with ease.

Thursday, August 15 (Moon in Sagittarius)   The moon is in your sixth house today, Cancer. Keep up with your exercise regimen, and watch your diet. Attend to details related to your health; make a doctor or dentist appointment. Your personal health occupies your attention now. Help others, but don't deny your own needs.

Friday, August 16 (Moon into Capricorn, 10:26 p.m.) Venus moves into your fourth house today. Stay home this evening for a romantic interlude with your sweetheart. Domestic matters are highlighted. Take time to beautify your home with something new. You feel a close and loving tie to your roots.

Saturday, August 17 (Moon in Capricorn)   Yesterday's energy flows into your Saturday. You feel a strong desire to work with a partner now. You don't feel complete unless you and your partner or spouse are in tune. Avoid conflicts; go with the flow.

Sunday, August 18 (Moon into Aquarius, 11:07 p.m.) It's a number 9 day. Finish what you started. Visualize the future; set your goals, then make them so. Look beyond the immediate. Get ready for something new. Strive for universal appeal.

Monday, August 19 (Moon in Aquarius) The moon in your eighth house can affect your feelings about your belongings as well as things that you share with others, such as a spouse. You have a strong sense of duty and feel obligated to fulfill your promises. Security is an important issue with you right now.

Tuesday, August 20 (Moon into Pisces, 11:44 p.m.) With the full moon in your eighth house, you gain insight into a matter related to shared resources, an inheritance, or an insurance policy. You also better understand a metaphysical subject, such as life after death or astrology.

Wednesday, August 21 (Moon in Pisces) The feeling of security is an important issue with you right now. Your experiences are more intense than usual. You have a strong sense of duty and feel obligated to fulfill your promises. It's a good time to get involved in a cause aimed at improving life for large numbers of people.

Thursday, August 22 (Moon in Pisces) Imagination is highlighted. Watch for psychic events, synchronicities. Keep track of your dreams, including your daydreams. Ideas are ripe. It's a time for deep healing and inspiration.

Friday, August 23 (Moon into Aries, 2:13 a.m.) It's a number 5 day. Change and variety are highlighted. Think freedom; think outside the box. Eliminate any restrictions. Your creativity, personal grace, and magnetism are highlighted.

Saturday, August 24 (Moon in Aries)   The moon is in your tenth house today. Business or career matters are highlighted on this Saturday. You gain an elevation in prestige. You're more emotional and warm toward coworkers. You're also in the public eye now, so avoid any emotional displays. Be careful about crossing the line between your personal and professional lives.

Sunday, August 25 (Moon into Taurus, 8:14 a.m.) It's a number 7 day, your mystery day, Cancer. You work best on your own today. Knowledge is essential to success. Gather information, but don't make any absolute decisions until tomorrow. Go with the flow. Express your desires, but avoid self-deception.

Monday, August 26 (Moon in Taurus)   The moon is in your eleventh house today. Friends play an important role in your day, especially Scorpio and Pisces. While it was better for you to work on your own yesterday, today you find strength in numbers. You find meaning through friends and groups, especially a group of like-minded people working for the common good.

Tuesday, August 27 (Moon into Gemini, 6:08 p.m.) Mars moves into your sixth house today and stays there until October 15. You work hard to get things done. Be aware that coworkers might get annoyed by your aggressive behavior on the job. Control your temper. Don't be so concerned about details and getting everything perfect. It will all work out.

Wednesday, August 28 (Moon in Gemini)   The moon is in your twelfth house today. Unconscious attitudes can be difficult. Best to keep your feelings secret. It's a great day for a mystical or spiritual discipline. Your intuition is heightened.

Thursday, August 29 (Moon in Gemini) A change of scenery works to your advantage today. Contact with siblings, other relatives, or neighbors offers an opportunity to exchange new information. You see two sides of an issue now, Cancer. Get out, have fun, flirt.

Friday, August 30 (Moon into Cancer, 6:33 a.m.) It's a number 3 day. You can influence people now with your upbeat attitude. You're innovative and creative and communicate well. Enjoy the harmony, beauty, and pleasures of life. Remain flexible, warm, and receptive.

Saturday, August 31 (Moon in Cancer) The moon is in your first house today. You're feeling particularly sensitive. You're easily influenced by what others say, and you're also responsive to the way others relate to you. You're malleable and tend to change your mind on a whim now. You're dealing with your emotional self, the person you are becoming.

SEPTEMBER 2013

Sunday, September 1 (Moon into Leo, 7:02 p.m.) It's a number 2 day. That means that cooperation and partnership are highlighted again. There's a new beginning now, or a new opportunity arises. Your intuition focuses on relationships. Don't make waves. Don't rush or show resentment; let things develop.

Monday, September 2 (Moon in Leo)   The moon is in your second house today. You identify emotionally with your ideals now or whatever you value. You tend to equate your assets with emotional security. You feel best when surrounded by familiar objects, especially in your home. It's not the objects themselves that are important, but the feelings and memories you associate with them.

Tuesday, September 3 (Moon in Leo)   You're at center stage today, Cancer. Theatrics and drama are highlighted. Strut your stuff; showmanship is emphasized. You're impulsive and honest. Romance and love play a role.

Wednesday, September 4 (Moon into Virgo, 5:45 a.m.)   It's a number 5 day. Change and variety are highlighted now. Think freedom, no restrictions. Change your perspective. Approach the day with an unconventional mindset. Release old structures; get a new point of view. A change of scenery would work to your advantage.

Thursday, September 5 (Moon in Virgo)   There's a new moon in your third house today. New opportunities come your way related to your everyday world. You can expand whatever you're doing. You gain a better understanding of the details, especially those that relate to the past.

Friday, September 6 (Moon into Libra, 2:14 p.m.)
It's your mystery day, Cancer. You become aware of confidential information, secret meetings, things happening behind closed doors. You investigate like a detective solving a mystery. Dig deep and gather information, but don't act on what you learn until tomorrow.

Saturday, September 7 (Moon in Libra) The moon is in your fourth house, a comfortable place for you, Cancer. It's a good day to take off and stay home or work at home. Find time for a home-repair project. You could be dealing with parents now. You feel a close tie to your roots.

Sunday, September 8 (Moon into Scorpio, 8:45 p.m.)
It's a number 9 day. Clear your desk for tomorrow's new cycle. Accept what comes your way now, but don't start anything new today. Use the day for reflection, expansion, and concluding projects.

Monday, September 9 (Moon in Scorpio) Mercury moves into your fourth house today. There's strong mental activity in the home now, a high priority on learning. Home schooling a child is a possibility. Alternately, you're thinking a lot about your home, selling it or remodeling some aspect of it.

Tuesday, September 10 (Moon in Scorpio) You're emotionally in touch with your creative side now. There's also greater depth in a love relationship and more involvement with children and pets. You're emotionally tied to your children, but make sure you allow them room to grow.

Wednesday, September 11 (Moon into Sagittarius, 1:36 a.m.)   Venus moves into your fifth house today. That means you're very attractive to the opposite sex now and thrive on romantic attention. You also would enjoy visiting a museum or art gallery over the next three weeks. Others find you charming and easy-going.

Thursday, September 12 (Moon in Sagittarius) The moon is in your sixth house today. It's another service day, Cancer. If someone in your home environment could use your advice, be there for that person. Help others, but dance to your own tune. You improve, edit, and refine their work.

Friday, September 13 (Moon into Capricorn, 4:56 a.m.)   Change and variety are highlighted now. Think freedom; think outside the box. Your creativity, personal grace, and magnetism are highlighted. Get ready for changes. Promote new ideas; follow your curiosity. Look for adventure.

Saturday, September 14 (Moon in Capricorn)   The moon is in your seventh house today. You get along well with others now. You can fit in just about anywhere. Loved ones and partners are more important than usual. You comprehend the nuances of a situation, but it's difficult to go with the flow. Be careful that others don't manipulate your feelings.

Sunday, September 15 (Moon into Aquarius, 7:06 a.m.)   It's a number 7 day. Knowledge is essential to success. You investigate, analyze, or simply observe what's going on. Gather information, but don't make any absolute decisions until tomorrow. Go with the flow.

Monday, September 16 (Moon in Aquarius) The moon is in your eighth house today. Your experiences are more intense than usual. You could be exploring a metaphysical matter, such as life after death or psychic abilities. Your intuition is strong. Security is an important issue now. You could be managing resources that you share with others.

Tuesday, September 17 (Moon into Pisces, 8:59 a.m.) It's a number 9 day. Clear up odds and ends. Accept what comes your way, but don't start anything new. It's all part of a cycle. Use the day for reflection, expansion, and concluding projects. Strive for universal appeal.

Wednesday, September 18 (Moon in Pisces) The moon is in your ninth house today, the home of higher learning. You're full of ideas now on matters such as philosophy or religion, the law or publishing. You also have a strong interest in foreign travel or a foreign nation. It's a good time to look to the big picture, Cancer. Break away from your routine or the usual way you think about things.

Thursday, September 19 (Moon into Aries, 11:58 a.m.) There's a full moon in your ninth house today. Now you have an opportunity to clarify and expand what you were working on or thinking about yesterday. You gain a better understanding of a matter related to higher education or long-distance travel.

Friday, September 20 (Moon in Aries)   Pluto goes direct in your seventh house today, where it will remain until 2024. That releases more energy for a partnership or marriage. You could be dealing with a new contract or contracts. You're moving forward and outward. A partnership plays a role. Keep in mind that Pluto transforms everything that is not needed.

Saturday, September 21 (Moon into Taurus, 5:34 p.m.)   It's a good day to get organized. Clean out your garage, attic, or closet. Tear down the old in order to rebuild. Be methodical and thorough. Missing papers are found. Revise and rewrite. You're building a creative base.

Sunday, September 22 (Moon in Taurus)   The moon is in your eleventh house today. Friends play an important role in your day, especially Scorpio and Pisces. You work well with others, especially in a group. Focus on your wishes and dreams. Examine your overall goals, and make sure that they're still an expression of who you are.

Monday, September 23 (Moon in Taurus)   You're feeling strong-willed today. Be aware that you might be somewhat stubborn and resistant to change. Health and physical activity are highlighted. It's a good time for cultivating ideas, but make sure that they're practical.

Tuesday, September 24 (Moon into Gemini, 2:35 a.m.)   It's a number 7 day. Secrets, intrigue, confidential information play a role today. You might feel best working on your own. You investigate, analyze, or simply observe what's going on now. You quickly come to a conclusion and wonder why others don't see what you see. It's best to hold off on making any final decisions for a couple of days.

Wednesday, September 25 (Moon in Gemini)   The moon is in your twelfth house today. Think carefully before you act. There's a tendency now to undo all the positive actions you've taken. Avoid any self-destructive behavior. Be aware of hidden enemies. You might feel a need to withdraw and work on your own.

Thursday, September 26 (Moon into Cancer, 2:25 p.m.)   Look beyond the immediate. Finish what you started. Make room for something new. Take an inventory on where things are going in your life. It's a good day to make a donation to a worthy cause.

Friday, September 27 (Moon in Cancer)   With the moon in your first house today, Cancer, your thoughts and emotions are aligned. You could feel somewhat moody, shifting from happy one moment, sad the next, then back again. You're dealing with your self-awareness, your appearance, and the person you are becoming.

Saturday, September 28 (Moon in Cancer)   The moon is on your ascendant today, and you're recharged for the month ahead. This makes you more appealing to the public. The way you see yourself now is the way others see you. Your face is in front of the public now. You're restless, impulsive, and inquisitive. Worldviews arise.

Sunday, September 29 (Moon into Leo, 2:58 a.m.) Mercury moves into your fifth house today. You communicate well, especially with a lover. You get your message across. Alternately, you could feel strongly about a creative project you're working on or about a child or children.

Monday, September 30 (Moon in Leo) The moon is in your second house today. Money and material goods are important to you now and give you a sense of security. You identify emotionally with your possessions or whatever you value. Watch your spending.

OCTOBER 2013

Tuesday, October 1 (Moon into Virgo, 1:53 p.m.) Your attitude determines everything today. Spread your good news, and take time to listen to others. You will find that if you allow yourself free time to pursue a creative project, then your spirits will soar as will your productivity.

Wednesday, October 2 (Moon in Virgo) The moon is in your third house today. As you go about your everyday life, look to the past for clues about what's coming up in the near future. Your mental abilities are strong now, and you have an emotional need to reinvigorate your studies, especially regarding matters of the past. You also could be getting involved in a challenging mental activity, such as on-line gaming, a debate, or a game of chess, anything that calls for your mental prowess.

Thursday, October 3 (Moon into Libra, 10:00 p.m.) You're restless and looking for change, a new perspective. You're versatile and changeable, but be careful not to overcommit yourself now. Take risks, experiment, and pursue a new idea. Freedom of thought and action is key.

Friday, October 4 (Moon in Libra)   There's a new moon in your fourth house today. You're dealing with the foundations of who you are and who you are becoming. You get a fresh start on your domestic life. That could mean a move or a renovation of your home. Alternately, you revitalize contact with your roots, either parents or friends from childhood.

Saturday, October 5 (Moon in Libra)   Yesterday's energy flows into your Saturday with the focus on the domestic scene. You feel close to your family, your home, your property. Work on a home-repair project. Beautify your home. But also take time to retreat to a special private place for meditation.

Sunday, October 6 (Moon into Scorpio, 3:33 a.m.) It's your power day and your day to play it your way. Be flexible, and look for a new approach that could bring in big bucks. Remember you're playing with power, so be careful not to hurt others.

Monday, October 7 (Moon in Scorpio)   Venus moves into your sixth house today. You take great pleasure in the workplace this month. You get along well with coworkers and offer your assistance. You also feel good about your health situation and your diet.

Tuesday, October 8 (Moon into Sagittarius, 7:22 a.m.)   It's a number 1 day. You're at the top of your cycle. Get out and meet new people, have new experiences. Do something that you've never done before. In romance something new is developing. Stress originality. Refuse to deal with people who have closed minds.

Wednesday, October 9 (Moon in Sagittarius)   The moon is in your sixth house today. It's another service day. However, you could be feeling sensitive now and emotionally down. Help others where you can, but avoid falling into a martyr syndrome. Take time to exercise, and eat healthy meals. Get ready for a fun day tomorrow.

Thursday, October 10 (Moon into Capricorn, 10:18 a.m.)   Take time to relax, enjoy yourself, recharge your batteries. You can influence people now with your upbeat attitude. Play your hunches. In business dealings, diversify now. Insist on all the information, not just bits and pieces.

Friday, October 11 (Moon in Capricorn)   The moon is in your seventh house today. You get along well with others now. You can fit in just about anywhere. Loved ones and partners are more important than usual. You focus on how the public relates to you.

You feel a need to be accepted. You're looking for security, but you have a hard time going with the flow.

Saturday, October 12 (Moon into Aquarius, 1:00 p.m.) Approach the day with an unconventional mindset. Experiment; promote new ideas. You're feeling versatile and changeable today, but be careful not to diversify too much. You'll be in a hurry all day, so watch your step.

Sunday, October 13 (Moon in Aquarius) The moon is in your eighth house today. You could attract the attention of powerful people. Your experiences could be more intense than usual. Matters related to shared belongings, investments, taxes, or insurance could play a role. A metaphysical subject, such as life after death or astrology, catches your attention.

Monday, October 14 (Moon into Pisces, 4:06 p.m.) Get ready for a journey into the unknown. Secrets, intrigue, confidential information play a role. Knowledge is essential to success. Gather information, but avoid making any absolute decisions for the time being. You work best on your own today.

Tuesday, October 15 (Moon in Pisces) Mars moves into your third house today. You're more aggressive in pursuing your everyday activities over the next three weeks. You could be confronting a matter from the past. Be aware of your tendencies during this time to act more confrontational than usual, Cancer.

That's especially true when dealing with siblings, other relatives, or neighbors.

Wednesday, October 16 (Moon into Aries, 8:19 p.m.)
It's a number 9 day. Complete a project now. Make room for something new. Visualize the future; set your goals, then make them so. Strive for universal appeal. Spiritual values surface.

Thursday, October 17 (Moon in Aries)   The moon is in your tenth house today. It's a good day for dealing with the public, Cancer. Your thoughts and especially your feelings are more exposed. You're more responsive to the needs and moods of a group and the public in general. You gain an elevation in prestige.

Friday, October 18 (Moon in Aries)   There's a lunar eclipse in your tenth house today. That means you react emotionally to an event related to your professional life. Whatever is happening, you gain insight that can help you move ahead in your career.

Saturday, October 19 (Moon into Taurus, 2:28 a.m.)
It's a number 3 day. Your charm and wit are appreciated. You're curious and inventive now. Take time to relax and get your batteries recharged. In romance you are ardent and feeling loyal to your partner.

Sunday, October 20 (Moon in Taurus)   The moon is in your eleventh house today. Friends play an important role in your day, especially Pisces and Scorpio. You find strength in numbers. Focus on your wishes and dreams. Examine your overall goals. Those goals should be an expression of who you are.

Monday, October 21 (Moon into Gemini, 11:15 a.m.)   Mercury goes retrograde in your fifth house today and stays that way until November 10. That means you can expect some delays and glitches in communication over the next three weeks, especially related to children or a creative project. Expect some confusion in dealings with a romantic partner as well. He or she might misinterpret your intentions. It's best to relax and control your emotional reactions to situations now.

Tuesday, October 22 (Moon in Gemini)   The moon is in your twelfth house today, Cancer. Unconscious attitudes can be difficult. Keep your feelings secret. You might feel a need to withdraw and work on your own. Take time to reflect and meditate. It's a great time for pursuing a spiritual discipline.

Wednesday, October 23 (Moon into Cancer, 10:37 p.m.)   It's a number 7 day. Secrets, intrigue, confidential information play a role. Gather information, but don't make any absolute decisions until tomorrow. You investigate, analyze, or simply observe what's going on now. You quickly come to a conclusion and wonder why others don't see what you see. You detect deception and recognize insincerity with ease.

Thursday, October 24 (Moon in Cancer)   The moon is in your first house today, Cancer. Domestic matters play a big role in your day, especially related to your feelings about your home life. It's all about your emotional self. Your thoughts and feelings are aligned. Self-awareness and appearance are important now.

Friday, October 25 (Moon in Cancer)   With the moon in your first house and on your ascendant, you get your batteries recharged. You're physically vital, Cancer, and get along well with the opposite sex. You're also malleable and easily change your mind now. You're restless and uncertain which direction to proceed.

Saturday, October 26 (Moon into Leo, 11:13 a.m.) You're at the top of your cycle again. Be independent, creative, and refuse to be discouraged by naysayers. Take the lead, get a fresh start, a new beginning. Don't be afraid to turn in a new direction. Trust your hunches; intuition is highlighted.

Sunday, October 27 (Moon in Leo)   The moon is in your second house today. Finances and money issues take center stage now, Cancer. You identify emotionally with your possessions or whatever you value. Watch your spending. You feel best when surrounded by familiar objects, especially in your home environment. It's not the objects themselves that are important, but the feelings and memories you associate with them. Put off making any major purchases.

Monday, October 28 (Moon into Virgo, 10:45 p.m.) Your charm and wit are appreciated. You're curious and inventive. Take time to relax and get your batteries recharged. In romance you are ardent and feeling loyal to your partner. The social energy of the day is warm and welcoming.

Tuesday, October 29 (Moon in Virgo)   The moon is in your third house today, Cancer. You get your ideas across, but try not to get too emotional, especially with siblings and neighbors. A female relative plays an important role. Follow your hunches. You write from a deep place.

Wednesday, October 30 (Moon in Virgo)   Take care of details now; read the fine print. You might find that your colleagues are speeding ahead of you while you are stuck rechecking, revising, or editing. Take your time, and proceed at your own pace. Don't let the pace of others intimidate you. Also, pay attention to any health or diet issue.

Thursday, October 31 (Moon into Libra, 7:22 a.m.)   It's a number 6 day. Service to others is the theme of the day. Offer your advice and support. Diplomacy wins the way. Be sympathetic and kind, generous and tolerant.

NOVEMBER 2013

Friday, November 1 (Moon in Libra)   You're busy keeping your mind occupied with new information. Take what you know, and share it with others. Your communications with others are subjective, so keep conscious control of your emotions when speaking. Your thinking is unduly influenced by things of the past.

Saturday, November 2 (Moon into Scorpio, 1:35 p.m.) A change of scenery would work to your advantage. You could be moving to a new location. You can overcome obstacles with ease. It's a good time for travel, adventure, and meeting new people. You're seeking new horizons, but you tend to lack order and discipline.

Sunday, November 3—Daylight Saving Time Ends (Moon in Scorpio) There's a solar eclipse in your fifth house today. That means new opportunities come your way related to a creative project that could involve children. With four planets also in Scorpio, everything is enhanced—for better or worse—especially your personal health. It's the beginning or end of something that could be related to a romantic alliance.

Monday, November 4 (Moon into Sagittarius, 3:14 p.m.) It's a number 7 day. Secrets, intrigue, confidential information play a role. You investigate, analyze, or simply observe what's going on now. You quickly come to a conclusion and wonder why others don't see what you see. You detect deception and recognize insincerity with ease. Gather information, but don't make any absolute decisions until tomorrow.

Tuesday, November 5 (Moon in Sagittarius) Venus moves into your seventh house today. For the rest of the month you'll get along well with a partner in either a personal or business relationship. You see eye to eye and you feel close to each other. A contract could be involved, and you gain in status as a result.

Wednesday, November 6 (Moon into Capricorn, 4:44 p.m.)   It's a number 9 day, a good day to complete a project and get ready for a fresh start. Accept what comes your way now. It's all part of a cycle. Use the day for reflection, expansion, and concluding projects. Don't start anything new today.

Thursday, November 7 (Moon in Capricorn)   With Jupiter going direct in your first house today, you have an opportunity to expand your personal life into new areas. Your thoughts and emotions are aligned, and you see the big picture. You feel that anything is possible now.

Friday, November 8 (Moon into Aquarius, 6:31 p.m.)   It's a number 2 day. Cooperation and partnerships are highlighted. Your intuition focuses on relationships. You're diplomatic and capable of fixing whatever has gone wrong. You excel in working with others. You're playing the role of the visionary today.

Saturday, November 9 (Moon in Aquarius)   The moon is in your eighth house today. You feel a need to help others, but your own security is also important. You could be managing other people's resources now. You take a renewed interest in a metaphysical subject, such as astrology.

Sunday, November 10 (Moon into Pisces, 9:37 p.m.)   Mercury goes direct in your fifth house today. Misunderstandings and miscommunication with a romantic partner recede into the past. Also, you can move ahead with a creative project. You get along better with any children in your life. The delays and confusion are over.

Monday, November 11 (Moon in Pisces)   The moon is in your ninth house today, the home of higher learning. You communicate well now. Ideas and philosophies are important, especially those that help you advance in your plans, Cancer. It's a good day to prepare for a trip or sign up for a seminar or workshop. A foreign country or person of foreign birth could play a role. Publicity and advertising are emphasized.

Tuesday, November 12 (Moon in Pisces)   It's a good day to escape from the usual routine and the drudgery, Cancer. You're a dreamer *and* a thinker today, but now you're ready for action. You're restless and yearn for a new experience, and now you have the energy to follow through. Plan a long trip. Sign up for a workshop or seminar.

Wednesday, November 13 (Moon into Aries, 2:40 a.m.)   With Neptune going direct in your ninth house today, you could be working on your belief system. You're looking for the ideal situation in higher education or long-distance travel. It's a great time for initiating projects, launching new ideas, brainstorming.

Thursday, November 14 (Moon in Aries)   With the moon in your tenth house today, you communicate your feelings well to coworkers, who are sympathetic. You're looking for a raise or an advancement; you know you deserve it. Your life is more public now. It's a good day for sales, dealing with the public.

Friday, November 15 (Moon into Taurus, 9:50 a.m.)
Complete a project now, and take an inventory on where things are going in your life. Clear your desk for tomorrow's new cycle. Accept what comes your way, but don't start anything new until tomorrow.

Saturday, November 16 (Moon in Taurus) The moon is in your eleventh house today. You work well with group of like-minded individuals. You find strength in numbers. At the same time your individuality is stressed. Focus on your wishes and dreams. Examine your overall goals. Those goals should be an expression of who you are. Social consciousness plays a role in your day.

Sunday, November 17 (Moon into Gemini, 7:08 p.m.) There's a full moon in your eleventh house today. Friends play an important role. You reap what you've sown related to your wishes and dreams. You gain a better understanding of your relationships with friends and associates. You work well with a group of like-minded people.

Monday, November 18 (Moon in Gemini) The moon is in your twelfth house today. Think carefully before you act or speak. Consider: is it kind, is it true, is it necessary? If you're not careful, there's a tendency now to undo all the positive actions you've taken. You might feel a need to withdraw. Take time to reflect and meditate.

Tuesday, November 19 (Moon in Gemini) Imagination is highlighted. Watch for psychic events, synchronicities. Keep track of your dreams, including your daydreams. Ideas are ripe. You can tap deeply into the collective unconscious for inspiration. Universal knowledge, eternal truths, deep spirituality are the themes of the day.

Wednesday, November 20 (Moon into Cancer, 6:24 a.m.) Promote new ideas now; follow your curiosity. Freedom of thought and action is key. Think outside the box. Take risks; experiment. Variety is the spice of life.

Thursday, November 21 (Moon in Cancer) The moon is on your ascendant. The way you see yourself now is the way others see you. You're recharged for the remainder of the month, and this makes you more appealing to the public. You're physically vital, and relations with the opposite sex go well.

Friday, November 22 (Moon into Leo, 6:57 p.m.) It's a number 7 day. Secrets, intrigue, confidential information play a role. You investigate, analyze, or simply observe what's going on now. You quickly come to a conclusion and wonder why others don't see what you see. You detect deception and recognize insincerity with ease. Gather information, but don't make any absolute decisions until tomorrow.

Saturday, November 23 (Moon in Leo) Expect emotional experiences related to money today. You equate your financial assets with emotional security now. Watch how you spend your money, and make sure you have your priorities correct. Money and material goods give you a sense of security.

Sunday, November 24 (Moon in Leo) You're at center stage today, Cancer. Drama is highlighted. You feel like flaunting and celebrating. Be wild, imaginative; be the person you always imagined you might be. Play with different personae.

Monday, November 25 (Moon into Virgo, 7:11 a.m.) It's a number 1 day, and that means you're at the top of your cycle. You get a fresh start, a new beginning. You can take the lead now, and don't be afraid to turn in a new direction. Stress originality in whatever you're doing.

Tuesday, November 26 (Moon in Virgo) The moon is in your third house today. It's a good day for expressing yourself through writing. Take what you know, and share it with others. As you go about your daily life, look for ways to succeed in whatever you're doing. Expect an invitation to a social event.

Wednesday, November 27 (Moon into Libra, 5:00 p.m.) Ease up on your routines. Your attitude determines everything today. Take time to relax, enjoy yourself, recharge your batteries. You can influence people now with your upbeat attitude. In romance you're an ardent and loyal lover.

Thursday, November 28 (Moon in Libra) The moon is in your fourth house today. Spend time with your family and other loved ones. Stick close to home. You're dealing with the foundations of who you are and who you are becoming. It's a good day for meditation and dream recall. Happy Thanksgiving.

Friday, November 29 (Moon into Scorpio, 11:04 p.m.)   It's a number 5 day. Change and variety are highlighted now. Think freedom, no restrictions. Release old structures; get a new point of view. You're versatile and changeable, but be careful not to spread out and diversify too much.

Saturday, November 30 (Moon in Scorpio)   The moon is in your fifth house today. Your emotions tend to overpower your intellect. You're emotionally in touch with your creative side now. Be yourself; be emotionally honest. In love there's greater emotional depth to a relationship. Try not to be overly possessive of loved ones.

DECEMBER 2013

Sunday, December 1 (Moon in Scorpio)   The moon is in your fifth house. Your emotions tend to overpower your intellect today. Be yourself; be emotionally honest. In love there's greater emotional depth to a relationship now. You're also emotionally in touch with your creative side.

Monday, December 2 (Moon into Sagittarius, 1:32 a.m.)   There's a new moon today in your sixth house. New opportunities come your way related to your daily work. A new doorway opens. Others rely on you now. You're the one they go to for help. It's a good day to take care of any health issues. There could be something new available for you related to a health matter.

Tuesday, December 3 (Moon in Sagittarius)   The moon is in your sixth house. You could be feeling somewhat emotionally repressed today. Help others where you can, but attend to your own concerns as well. Keep your resolutions about exercise. Pay particular attention to diet and nutrition.

Wednesday, December 4 (Moon into Capricorn, 1:51 a.m.)   Mercury moves into your sixth house today. You're methodical and thorough now; you like everything in order. You're thinking about your health and physical well-being, but it's not an emotional issue. It's a good time to make an appointment for a physical or discuss any concerns with your doctor. You communicate well and get your ideas across, especially when you're helping others.

Thursday, December 5 (Moon in Capricorn)   The moon is in your seventh house today. The focus turns to relationships, both personal and business. You communicate smoothly and get along well with others now. You can fit in just about anywhere. You comprehend the nuances of a situation.

Friday, December 6 (Moon into Aquarius, 1:55 a.m.)   It's a number 1 day, and you're at the top of your cycle. Be independent and creative. Don't let others tell you what to do. Get out and meet new people, have new experiences, do something you've never done before. Express your opinions dynamically.

Saturday, December 7 (Moon in Aquarius)   Mars moves into your fourth house today. You're strongly focused on your home life. You can accomplish a lot now. Work on a home-repair project. Beautify your surroundings. Try not to be overly aggressive; avoid being a disruptive force.

Sunday, December 8 (Moon into Pisces, 3:35 a.m.) It's a number 3 day. You come out of your shell now. You communicate well. You're warm and receptive to what others say. Spread your good news. Ease up on routines. Your charm and wit are appreciated. Play your hunches.

Monday, December 9 (Moon in Pisces) The moon is in your ninth house today. You're a dreamer and a thinker. You impart knowledge and guide others in their intellectual development. It's a good time to plan a long journey, especially if you're feeling restless. You yearn for new experiences. A foreign destination or a foreign-born person plays a role.

Tuesday, December 10 (Moon into Aries, 8:06 a.m.) It's a number 5 day. Change your perspective. Approach the day with an unconventional mindset. (Easier said than done!) Think outside the box. Variety is the spice of life. Take risks; experiment. Get ready for change.

Wednesday, December 11 (Moon in Aries) The moon is in your tenth house today. Your life is more public. You gain an elevation in prestige, related to your profession or whatever you do. You're more responsive to the needs and moods of a group and the public in general.

Thursday, December 12 (Moon into Taurus, 3:41 p.m.)   Secrets, intrigue, confidential information play a role today. You might feel best working on your own. You investigate, analyze, or simply observe what's going on now. You quickly come to a conclusion and wonder why others don't see what you see. It's best to hold off on making any final decisions for a couple of days.

Friday, December 13 (Moon in Taurus)   The moon is in your eleventh house today. You get along especially well with friends and members of a group. You work for the common good, but keep an eye on your own wishes and dreams. Your sense of security is tied to your relationships and friends.

Saturday, December 14 (Moon in Taurus)   Cultivate new ideas, but make sure that they're down-to-earth. It's a good day to use common sense and take a down-to-earth perspective on whatever you're doing. You're feeling sensual and opinionated today, but you also might tend to be somewhat stubborn if someone disagrees with you.

Sunday, December 15 (Moon into Gemini, 1:41 a.m.) You're at the top of your cycle again. Be independent and creative. Don't let others tell you what to do. Get out and meet new people, have new experiences, do something you've never done before. Express your opinions dynamically.

Monday, December 16 (Moon in Gemini)   The moon is in your twelfth house today. After your busy

Sunday, it's a good day to withdraw and work behind the scenes. You might communicate your deepest feelings to a friend, but otherwise keep your thoughts to yourself. Take time to reflect and meditate. Sort out all the chaos; put your plans together.

Tuesday, December 17 (Moon into Cancer, 1:17 p.m.) With Uranus going direct in your tenth house today, you feel a strong need to work smoothly with fellow workers. Just make sure you receive the recognition that you deserve. There's also a full moon in your twelfth house, which suggests that you gain insight into a matter from the deep past. Take time again to reflect and meditate.

Wednesday, December 18 (Moon in Cancer) With the moon on your ascendant, you get your batteries recharged. You're physically vital, Cancer, and get along well with the opposite sex. You're also malleable and easily change your mind now. You're restless and uncertain what to do.

Thursday, December 19 (Moon in Cancer) With the moon in your first house today, your thoughts and feelings are aligned. Others see you as you see yourself. You're feeling vital now. It's all about your health and your emotional self: how you feel and how you feel about yourself. You tend to search for ways to improve yourself.

Friday, December 20 (Moon into Leo, 1:48 a.m.) You're creative and passionate today, impulsive and honest. Focus on making people happy today. Do a good deed for someone. Be sympathetic, kind, and compassionate. However, avoid scattering your energies.

Saturday, December 21 (Moon in Leo) Venus goes retrograde in your seventh house today and stays that way until January 31. It's not a good time to get married or form a business partnership. You could have problems getting along and general disagreements. You also might have second thoughts later about any contracts you sign during this time.

Sunday, December 22 (Moon into Virgo, 2:20 p.m.) It's a number 8 day, your power day, Cancer. Speculate, take a chance. Focus on a power play. Open your mind to a new approach that could bring in big bucks. Be aware that fear of failure or fear that you won't measure up might attract exactly that experience. Unexpected money comes your way.

Monday, December 23 (Moon in Virgo) The moon is in your third house today. You're moving about in your everyday world handling chores. You're talking with close family, other relatives, and neighbors, getting your ideas across. You look to the past for inspiration. Try to control your emotions when dealing with siblings. Be particularly cautious if you're driving and talking on your cell phone.

Tuesday, December 24 (Moon in Virgo) Mercury moves into your seventh house today. You could find yourself serving as an arbitrator between two factions.

You tend to deal with intelligent and articulate people now. A partnership plays a role. You get your ideas across.

Wednesday, December 25 (Moon into Libra, 1:18 a.m.) Cooperation is key today. A partnership plays an important role in your day. That's been the case all week. Be kind and understanding. Family members play a role. Best not to make waves now; go with the flow. Merry Christmas!

Thursday, December 26 (Moon in Libra) The moon is in your fourth house today. A love matter needs special attention. You're dealing with the foundations of who you are and who you are becoming. Best to stay home with your partner rather than go out with friends tonight. A parent plays a role. It's a good day for dream recall.

Friday, December 27 (Moon into Scorpio, 8:59 a.m.) It's a number 4 day. Tear down the old in order to re-build. Be methodical and thorough. Your organizational skills are highlighted. Control your impulses to wander off task. You're building a creative base for your future.

Saturday, December 28 (Moon in Scorpio) The moon is in your fifth house today. Be yourself; be emotionally honest. In love there's greater emotional depth to a relationship now. You're emotionally in touch with your creative side. It's a good day to take a chance, experiment.

Sunday, December 29 (Moon into Sagittarius, 12:38 p.m.) It's a service day. Do a good deed for someone. Visit someone who is ill or in need of help. You're passionate but impatient. Be understanding, and avoid confrontations.

Monday, December 30 (Moon in Sagittarius) The moon is in your sixth house today. It's another service day. Others come to you for help. You improve and refine what they started. Offer assistance, but don't deny your own needs. Take care of any health issues.

Tuesday, December 31 (Moon into Capricorn, 1:02 p.m.) It's a number 8 day, a good day to buy a lotto ticket. It's your power day, your day to play it your way. You can go far with your plans and achieve financial success. Unexpected money comes your way.

HAPPY NEW YEAR!

JANUARY 2014

Wednesday, January 1 (Moon in Capricorn) The year begins with a new moon and five planets in your seventh house. That means new opportunities come your way today related to partnerships. Loved ones and partners take on significance as they come to your support. Your emotions are strong, and you could be celebrating opportunities that come to you through a partnership. A contract could be involved. Look for a new beginning on this New Year's Day.

Thursday, January 2 (Moon into Aquarius, 12:04 p.m.)   Promote new ideas; follow your curiosity today, Cancer. Release old structures; get a new point of view. Think outside the box. Freedom of thought and action is key. You can easily overcome obstacles.

Friday, January 3 (Moon in Aquarius)   With the moon in your eighth house today, you have a strong sense of duty and willingness to help others. You're curious now about a social movement, and you might join such an effort. Your experiences are more intense than usual, and you might take an interest in exploring some of the deeper mysteries of life.

Saturday, January 4 (Moon into Pisces, 11:59 a.m.) It's a number 7 day. You work best on your own today as you journey into unexplored territory. Secrets, intrigue, confidential information play a role. You investigate, analyze, or simply observe what's going on now. Gather information, but don't make any absolute decisions until tomorrow.

Sunday, January 5 (Moon in Pisces)   Issues of the day include an interest or plans for a long-distance trip, pursuing higher education, or exploring the higher mind. You could take an interest in studying in a foreign land, or maybe you meet a foreign-born person today.

Monday, January 6 (Moon into Aries, 2:46 p.m.) It's a number 9 day. Visualize the future; set your goals, then make them so. Look beyond the immediate. Complete a project; clear up odds and ends. Take an inventory on where things are going in your life. It's a good day to make a donation to a worthy cause.

Tuesday, January 7 (Moon in Aries)　The moon is in your tenth house today. You communicate your feelings well to coworkers, who are sympathetic. You get along well with others in the workplace. Your life is more public now, so take care to avoid emotional displays.

Wednesday, January 8 (Moon into Taurus, 9:24 p.m.) Use your intuition to get a sense of your day. Partnerships continue to play an important role this month. Cooperation is highlighted. Be kind and understanding. Don't make waves today.

Thursday, January 9 (Moon in Taurus)　The moon is in your eleventh house today. You have deeper contact with friends now. You find strength in numbers and meaning through relationships. You work for the common good. Scorpio and Pisces play a role in your day.

Friday, January 10 (Moon in Taurus)　Under the influence of the Taurus moon, your health and physical activity are highlighted. Go to the gym or a yoga studio. It's a good time for doing practical things, cultivating ideas. Try to avoid stubborn behavior when others question your actions. You could be somewhat possessive now. While you maintain a common-sense, down-to-earth perspective on life, you also long for the good life with its material blessings.

Saturday, January 11 (Moon into Gemini, 7:26 a.m.)
As Mercury enters your eighth house, you're follow-ing your curiosity, promoting new ideas, and looking for adventure. You dig deep for answers. A matter re-lated to joint resources comes to your attention. It could involve taxes, finances, or insurance. You might also investigate the deeper mysteries of life.

Sunday, January 12 (Moon in Gemini)   With the moon in your twelfth house today, you feel a need to withdraw and work behind the scenes. It's a great day for pursuing a spiritual discipline. There's a tendency towards secrecy and difficult dealings with others, es-pecially women.

Monday, January 13 (Moon into Cancer, 7:25 p.m.)
You launch a journey into the unknown; you pursue a mystery. Dig deep and look behind closed doors. You quickly come to a conclusion and wonder why others don't see what you see. Confidential information, se-crets are involved.

Tuesday, January 14 (Moon in Cancer)   With the moon on your ascendant today, the way you see your-self is the way others see you. You're recharged for the remainder of the month, and you're more appealing to the public. Relations with the opposite sex go well. You're feeling physically vital, and your thoughts and emotions are aligned.

Wednesday, January 15 (Moon in Cancer)   There's a full moon in your first house today with Saturn forming a beneficial angle. You reap what you've sown related to your personal life. You communicate well and get your message across, Cancer. You're more serious and responsible in dealing with your health and personal life. Your self-awareness and appearance are important. You're dealing with the person you are becoming. That's not a passing theme, but one that will remain with you for months to come.

Thursday, January 16 (Moon into Leo, 8:01 a.m.)
It's a number 1 day, Cancer, and you're at the top of your cycle again. Be independent, creative, and refuse to be discouraged by naysayers. Trust your hunches; intuition is highlighted. You get a fresh start, and don't be afraid to turn in a new direction.

Friday, January 17 (Moon in Leo)   The moon is in your second house today, Cancer. Expect emotional experiences related to money. You identify emotionally with your possessions or whatever you value. It's not the objects themselves that are important, but your feelings related to them. Take care of any payments, and collect what's owed you.

Saturday, January 18 (Moon into Virgo, 8:25 p.m.)
It's a number 3 day. Take time to relax, enjoy yourself, recharge your batteries. You can influence people now with your upbeat attitude. Your charm and wit are appreciated. Foster generosity. In romance you're an ardent and loyal lover.

Sunday, January 19 (Moon in Virgo)   The moon is in your third house today. You could be getting involved in some sort of aggressive mental activities, such as on-line gaming, a debate, or a game of chess—anything that challenges your mental prowess. If you're in school, study for a test today and you'll do great on it tomorrow, especially if it's for a history class. Take what you know and share it, but don't expect others to be as excited as you are about delving into the past.

Monday, January 20 (Moon in Virgo) Under the influence of the Virgo moon, you feel an urge to exercise and watch your diet. Take care of details now, especially related to your health. Stop worrying and fretting. Take time to write in a journal. You write from a deep place with lots of details and colorful descriptions. Dig deep for information.

Tuesday, January 21 (Moon into Libra, 7:45 a.m.) It's a number 6 day. Focus on making people happy today. Be sympathetic, kind, and compassionate. Do a good deed for someone, but avoid scattering your energy. Dance to your own tune.

Wednesday, January 22 (Moon in Libra) The moon is in your fourth house today. It's a good day to stick close to home. Spend time with your family and loved ones. But also find time to focus inward in meditation. You feel a close tie to your roots. You could be dealing with your parents now.

Thursday, January 23 (Moon into Scorpio, 4:45 p.m.) It's a number 8 day, your power day. Open your mind to a new approach that could bring in big bucks. Business discussions go well. You could pull off a financial coup now. You're playing with power, so be careful not to hurt others. You're being watched by people in power.

Friday, January 24 (Moon in Scorpio)   With the moon in your fifth house today, your emotions tend to overpower your intellect. You're emotionally in touch with your creative side. You're also more protective and nurturing toward children.

Saturday, January 25 (Moon into Sagittarius, 10:14 p.m.)   You're at the top of your cycle today. Be independent and creative and refuse to deal with nay-sayers. Stress originality. You're inventive and make connections that others overlook. You're determined and courageous. In romance something new is developing.

Sunday, January 26 (Moon in Sagittarius)   With the moon in your sixth house, your health occupies your attention now. Help others, but don't deny your own needs. Make any medical or dental appointments that you've been putting off. You get along well with friends in the workplace.

Monday, January 27 (Moon in Sagittarius)   Under the influence of the Sag moon, you see the big picture today, not just the details. You're restless and looking for ways to expand whatever you're doing, especially if it relates to travel or higher education. Worldviews are emphasized. Don't limit yourself. Keep track of your dreams, including your daydreams. Ideas are ripe.

Tuesday, January 28 (Moon into Capricorn, 12:05 a.m.)   Your organizational skills are highlighted. Persevere to get things done today. Control your impulses. Best to put romance on a back burner. Tear down the old in order to rebuild. Be methodical and thorough.

Wednesday, January 29 (Moon into Aquarius, 11:33 p.m.)   It's a number 5 day. Promote new ideas; follow your curiosity. Look for adventure. Change and variety are highlighted. Think freedom, no restrictions. Approach the day with an unconventional mind-set. You can overcome obstacles with ease.

Thursday, January 30 (Moon in Aquarius)   There's a new moon in your eighth house today, and that indicates a new opportunity related to shared income or resources. It could involve an inheritance, a mortgage, insurance, or taxes. You may feel a need to get away now, a break from the usual routine. You yearn for a new experience, especially one involving metaphysics. You might explore a subject such as astrology, reincarnation, or spirit contact. With Uranus forming a beneficial angle, whatever happens shakes you out of a rut. You embrace what's new and different.

Friday, January 31 (Moon into Pisces, 10:45 p.m.) Mercury moves into your ninth house today. You communicate well with others, especially when you're focused on higher education or plans for long-distance travel. A foreign-born person could play a role. With Venus going direct in your seventh house, you and a partner or love interest get along very well.

Saturday, February 1 (Moon in Pisces) The moon is in your ninth house today. Your mind is active, and you yearn for new experiences. You're playing with ideas now that could involve a foreign destination or a person of foreign origin. A long trip or a pursuit of higher education plays a role.

Sunday, February 2 (Moon into Aries, 11:55 p.m.) It's a number 6 day, a service day. Be diplomatic, especially with a person who is giving you trouble. Do a good deed for someone. Visit someone who is ill or in need of help. Be sympathetic, kind, and compassionate, but avoid scattering your energies.

Monday, February 3 (Moon in Aries) The moon is in your tenth house today. You're more responsive to the needs and moods of a group and of the public in general. Your life is more public, so avoid emotional displays. Try not to blur the boundary between your professional and private lives.

Tuesday, February 4 (Moon in Aries) Under the influence of the Aries moon, you get powered up for the rest of the month. It's a great day to brainstorm. You come up with new ideas. You're passionate but impatient. You're in the public eye and very persuasive, especially if you're passionate about what you're doing.

Wednesday, February 5 (Moon into Taurus, 4:47 a.m.) Complete a project now. Clear up odds and ends. Take an inventory on where things are going in your life. Clear your desk for tomorrow's new cycle. Accept what comes your way, but don't start anything new until tomorrow.

Thursday, February 6 (Moon in Taurus) Mercury turns retrograde in your ninth house today and stays there until February 28. That means there could be some miscommunication or misunderstanding over the next three weeks related to higher education. There could be delays and confusion in plans for long-distance travel or dealings with a foreign-born person. Make sure you read the fine print on any contracts.

Friday, February 7 (Moon into Gemini, 1:45 p.m.) It's a number 2 day. Use your intuition to get a sense of the day. Don't make waves. Don't rush or show resentment; let things develop. The spotlight is on cooperation. Show your appreciation to others.

Saturday, February 8 (Moon in Gemini) The moon is in your twelfth house today. Think carefully before you act. There's a tendency now to undo all the positive actions you've taken. You feel best working behind the scenes. Avoid any self-destructive behavior. Be aware of hidden enemies.

Sunday, February 9 (Moon in Gemini) Under the influence of the Gemini moon, you're feeling creative and needing to express yourself in writing. A change of scenery would do you good today, possibly a short trip to visit relatives. You might be in contact with siblings or in discussions with neighbors. You see two sides of an issue.

Monday, February 10 (Moon into Cancer, 1:34 a.m.)
It's a number 5 day. That means you're open to change and variety, and you desire to loosen any restrictions today. You're willing to take a risk and experiment. Variety is the spice of life, and change is good. Think outside the box.

Tuesday, February 11 (Moon in Cancer)   The moon is in your first house today, Cancer. Your self-awareness and appearance are important now. You're dealing with your emotional self, the person you are becoming. You might feel moody—happy one moment, sad or withdrawn the next. However, your thoughts and feelings are aligned. You tend to search for ways to improve yourself.

Wednesday, February 12 (Moon into Leo, 2:17 p.m.)
You launch a journey into the unknown today. Secrets, intrigue, confidential information play a role. Make sure that you see things as they are, not as you wish them to be. Express your desires, but avoid self-deception. Maintain your emotional balance.

Thursday, February 13 (Moon in Leo)   With the moon in your second house, money issues arise. You could get a quick financial boost today. It's a good time for investments. Look at your priorities in spending your income. Take care of payments and collections.

Friday, February 14 (Moon in Leo)   There's a full moon in your second house today. That means you can expect to hear news about finances or gain insight into your ideals or whatever you value. You tend to equate your financial assets with emotional security.

Saturday, February 15 (Moon into Virgo, 2:27 a.m.) It's a number 1 day, and you're at the top of your cycle again. Get out and meet new people, have new experiences, do something you've never done before. A flirtation could turn serious. You're inventive and make connections that others overlook. Stress originality, and avoid people with closed minds.

Sunday, February 16 (Moon in Virgo)   With the moon in your third house today, you're busy interacting with neighbors, relatives, or siblings in a social gathering. You get your ideas across in a big way, but try not to get too emotional, especially when you're talking about something from the past. A female relative plays an important role.

Monday, February 17 (Moon into Libra, 1:24 p.m.) It's a number 3 day. Your charm and wit are appreciated today. Make time to listen to others. Relax, enjoy yourself, recharge your batteries. In business dealings, diversify now. Insist on all the details, not just bits and pieces.

Tuesday, February 18 (Moon in Libra)   The moon is in your fourth house today. Spend time with your family and loved ones. A parent may play a role in your day. Take time to settle into a quiet place to meditate. You're dealing with the foundations of who you are and who you are becoming.

Wednesday, February 19 (Moon into Scorpio, 10:33 p.m.)   Promote new ideas; follow your curiosity. Approach the day with an unconventional outlook. Freedom of thought and action is key. You're versatile and changeable, Cancer. You're also courageous and adaptable. You can overcome obstacles with ease. Take risks; experiment.

Thursday, February 20 (Moon in Scorpio)   The moon is in your fifth house today. It's a great day for pursuing a creative project. Children play a role in your day. Your emotions tend to overpower your intellect. Be yourself; be emotionally honest. In love there's greater emotional depth to a relationship now. Sex for pleasure is highlighted.

Friday, February 21 (Moon in Scorpio)   Under the influence of the Scorpio moon, yesterday's emotional energy flows into your Friday. Your emotions grow intense as you investigate an important matter. Control issues arise. Be aware of things happening in secret. Forgive and forget; try to avoid going to extremes. You're also passionate today, and your sexuality is heightened.

Saturday, February 22 (Moon into Sagittarius, 5:12 a.m.)   It's a number 8 day, your power day and your day to play it your way. It's a good day to buy a lotto ticket. You can go far with your plans and achieve financial success. Unexpected money comes your way.

Sunday, February 23 (Moon in Sagittarius) The moon is in your sixth house today. It's a service-oriented day. Help others, but be careful not to fall into a martyr syndrome. Take care of health issues. It's a good time to begin a new diet or exercise regimen. Don't let your fears hold you back. You see the big picture now.

Monday, February 24 (Moon into Capricorn, 8:51 a.m.) Get out and meet new people, have new experiences, do something you've never done before. Explore and discover. Creativity is highlighted.

Tuesday, February 25 (Moon in Capricorn) The moon is in your seventh house today. You feel a strong desire to work with a partner now. You don't feel complete unless you and your partner or spouse are in tune. Avoid conflicts; go with the flow.

Wednesday, February 26 (Moon into Aquarius, 9:56 a.m.) Your charm and wit are appreciated today. You can influence people with your upbeat attitude. Take time to relax, enjoy yourself, recharge your batteries. Make time to listen to others. In romance you're an ardent lover.

Thursday, February 27 (Moon in Aquarius) With the moon in your eighth house today, you explore the deeper mysteries of life. Past lives and life after death are on your radar now. Your psychic abilities are highlighted. Issues of the day could include matters of sex, death, rebirth, rituals, and relationships.

Friday, February 28 (Moon into Pisces, 9:53 a.m.) Mercury goes direct in your eighth house today. That means any confusion, miscommunication, and delays that you've been experiencing recede into the past. Things move more smoothly now, especially related to shared finances and matters relating to insurance, a mortgage, taxes, or an inheritance.

MARCH 2014

Saturday, March 1 (Moon in Pisces) There's a new moon in your ninth house, which means new opportunities come your way related to higher education or long-distance travel. Meanwhile, Mars turns retrograde in your fourth house, where it stays until May 19. That suggests any aggressive actions you take related to renovations on your home will be met by delays and confusion. With Neptune forming a favorable conjunction, it's a good time for being with loved ones in your home.

Sunday, March 2 (Moon into Aries, 10:41 a.m.) Saturn turns retrograde in your fifth house today. You'll be thinking more about how you deal with a creative project. You're looking for stability, but it's slow in coming. By the time Saturn goes direct again July 20, you should be able to better integrate your ideas or concepts into a viable project.

Monday, March 3 (Moon in Aries) The moon is in your tenth house today. New opportunities arise related to your career. Professional concerns are the focus of the day as you pursue an elevation of prestige, raise, or promotion. You get along well with bosses and peers, but make sure that you don't get overly emotional in public.

Tuesday, March 4 (Moon into Taurus, 2:13 p.m.) It's a number 9 day. That means it's a good time to complete a project. Strive for universal appeal. Visualize the future; set your goals, then make them so. Spiritual values surface.

Wednesday, March 5 (Moon in Taurus) Venus moves into your eighth house today, where it stays until April 4. You gain through a partnership now. However, be careful not to get jealous or possessive. Things come to you easily. Alternately, you love pursuing a mystery, especially one that relates to past lives or life after death.

Thursday, March 6 (Moon into Gemini, 9:39 p.m.) Jupiter goes direct in your first house today. You're very competent and resourceful in dealing with personal matters. You're busy keeping your mind occupied with new information that might help you maintain or improve your health. You're also dealing with your emotional state today, which probably is focused on your personal issues.

Friday, March 7 (Moon in Gemini) The moon is in your twelfth house today. Unconscious attitudes can be difficult. So can relations with women. Keep your feelings to yourself now. Be aware of hidden enemies. It's a great day for a mystical or spiritual discipline. Your intuition is heightened.

Saturday, March 8 (Moon in Gemini)   Under the influence of the Gemini moon, you're mentally quick and communicate well. You see both sides of an issue. You're feeling creative and need to express yourself in writing. A change of scenery would do you good today, possibly a short trip to visit friends or relatives.

Sunday, March 9—Daylight Saving Time Begins (Moon into Cancer, 9:34 a.m.)   It's a number 5 day. That means you're open to change and variety, and you desire to loosen any restrictions today. You're willing to take a risk and experiment. Variety is the spice of life, and change works in your favor. Think outside the box.

Monday, March 10 (Moon in Cancer)   With the moon in your first house today, your self-awareness and appearance are important now. You're dealing with the person you are becoming. It's all about your health and emotional self: how you feel and how you feel about yourself. You're sensitive and responsive to the needs of others, so you're easily influenced by those around you.

Tuesday, March 11 (Moon into Leo, 10:10 p.m.) It's your mystery day, Cancer. Gather information, but don't make any absolute decisions until tomorrow. Knowledge is essential to success. Best to remain out of public view today. Go with the flow.

Wednesday, March 12 (Moon in Leo)   The moon is in your second house today, boding well for financial matters. Look at your priorities in handling your income. Take care of payments and collect what's owed you. You equate your financial assets with emotional security.

Thursday, March 13 (Moon in Leo)   Under the influence of the Leo moon, you're feeling particularly passionate today. You're impulsive and honest. Drama is highlighted; you're at center stage. It's a good day to dress boldly. Romance and love feel majestic. Let others know who you are.

Friday, March 14 (Moon into Virgo, 10:18 a.m.) Express your opinions dynamically. Get out and meet new people, have new experiences, do something you've never done before. You're determined and courageous today. You attract creative people now. Stress originality. In romance a flirtation turns more serious.

Saturday, March 15 (Moon in Virgo)   The moon is in your third house today. While you communicate well with family, relatives and neighbors, you tend to get emotional, Cancer, especially if you're dealing with matters from the past. Take care if you're driving and talking on your cell. Eyes on the road; hands on the wheel.

Sunday, March 16 (Moon into Libra, 8:46 p.m.) There's a full moon in your third house. You gain illumination and understanding related to matters of the past. Your mental abilities are strong now, and you have an emotional need to reinvigorate your studies, especially regarding matters of the past. You're attracted to historical or archaeological studies.

Monday, March 17 (Moon in Libra)   Mercury moves into your ninth house today, where it stays until April 7. You have lots of ideas during the next couple of weeks and the ability to express them well. It's a good time for teaching, writing, or learning a foreign language. Meanwhile, there's a full moon in your third house. You gain insight and illumination related to a matter from the past. You reap what you've sown. Siblings, other relatives, or neighbors play a role.

Tuesday, March 18 (Moon in Libra)   The moon is in your fourth house today. It's a good day to stick close to home. Take care of domestic issues. Spend time with your family. Work on a home-repair project or buy something for your home.

Wednesday, March 19 (Moon into Scorpio, 5:14 a.m.)   It's a number 6 day, a service day. Be understanding and avoid confrontations. Diplomacy and compassion win the way. Focus on making people happy, but avoid scattering your energies. Be sympathetic, kind, and understanding.

Thursday, March 20 (Moon in Scorpio)   The moon is in your fifth house today. Romance and sex for pleasure are highlighted. Your emotions tend to overpower your intellect now, and you're emotionally in touch with your creative side. You feel strongly attached to loved ones, particularly children.

Friday, March 21 (Moon into Sagittarius, 11:39 a.m.)   It's a number 8 day, your power day. Expect a financial coup. Open your mind to a new approach that will pay off. You have a chance to expand, to gain recognition, fame, power. You attract financial success.

Saturday, March 22 (Moon in Sagittarius)   The moon is in your sixth house today, and that means it's another service-oriented day. Help others, but be careful not to fall into a martyr syndrome. Take care of health issues. It's a good time to begin a new diet or exercise regimen. Don't let your fears hold you back.

Sunday, March 23 (Moon into Capricorn, 4:04 p.m.) It's a number 1 day. Get out and meet new people, have new experiences, do something you've never done before. Explore and discover. Creativity is highlighted. You're inventive and make connections that others overlook. In romance something new is developing.

Monday, March 24 (Moon in Capricorn)   The moon is in your seventh house today. You feel a strong desire to work with a partner now. You don't feel complete unless you and your partner or spouse are in tune. Avoid conflicts; go with the flow.

Tuesday, March 25 (Moon into Aquarius, 6:40 p.m.) Ease up on your routines. Your attitude determines everything today. Take time to relax, enjoy yourself, recharge your batteries. You can influence people now with your upbeat attitude.

Wednesday, March 26 (Moon in Aquarius)   The moon is in your eighth house today. Your experiences are more intense than usual, especially when dealing with matters related to your home. It's a good day to take time to meditate, especially at home, or study a metaphysical subject, such as life after death or reincarnation.

Thursday, March 27 (Moon into Pisces, 8:12 p.m.) It's a number 5 day. Promote new ideas; follow your curiosity. Freedom of thought and action is key. You're versatile and changeable today. You can overcome obstacles with ease. Take risks; experiment.

Friday, March 28 (Moon in Pisces)   The moon is in your ninth house today. You're a dreamer and thinker. You may feel a need to get away now, a break from the usual routine. You yearn for a new experience. It's a good time to plan a long trip or sign up for a workshop or seminar.

Saturday, March 29 (Moon into Aries, 9:55 p.m.) There's a sense of mystery in the air. You aggressively investigate, analyze, or just observe what's going on. Knowledge is essential to success. Gather information, but don't make any absolute decisions until tomorrow.

Sunday, March 30 (Moon in Aries)   There's a new moon in your tenth house, Cancer. That means new opportunities come your way related to your career. You get along well with others, especially coworkers. With Uranus closely conjunct, you might encounter sudden and unexpected changes related to your profession. Maintain your self-control, and try not to overextend yourself.

Monday, March 31 (Moon in Aries)   With the moon in your tenth house today, yesterday's energy flows into your Monday. You're ready for a boost in prestige, possibly a raise. You could be looking for a more public position. Friendly coworkers are on your side. Your life is more public today.

APRIL 2014

Tuesday, April 1 (Moon into Taurus, 1:21 a.m.) You're feeling sensitive, Cancer, and somewhat suspicious. You look behind closed doors today. Gather information, but don't make any absolute decisions until tomorrow. Go with the flow. Maintain your emotional balance, and avoid confusion and conflict.

Wednesday, April 2 (Moon in Taurus)   There's a new moon in your eleventh house today, and that suggests a new beginning or new opportunities. Friends play an important role, and you could be working with a group. You're in the driver's seat related to promotion and publicity. Power issues can surface now, but you're the one making the decisions.

Thursday, April 3 (Moon into Gemini, 7:49 a.m.) It's a number 9 day, a great time for completing projects and getting ready for something new. Clear up odds and ends. Take an inventory on where things are going in your life. Look beyond the present, but don't start anything new until tomorrow.

Friday, April 4 (Moon in Gemini) The moon is in your twelfth house today. You might feel a need to withdraw and work on your own. Things concerning the past, your childhood, play a role. You hide your emotions and moodiness. Take time to reflect and meditate.

Saturday, April 5 (Moon into Cancer, 5:40 p.m.) Venus moves into your ninth house today. Your intuition is highlighted. You could be launching an extended pleasure trip or at least planning one. Romance is in the air, and a foreign-born person or a foreign country could play a role. You enjoy studying philosophy and art, and you are open to people of different cultures and races.

Sunday, April 6 (Moon in Cancer) With the moon in your first house today, your feelings and thoughts are aligned. It's all about your health and emotional self: how you feel and how you feel about yourself. You are sensitive and responsive regarding the needs of others, so you are easily influenced by those around you. It's difficult to remain detached and objective now.

Monday, April 7 (Moon in Cancer) Mercury moves into your tenth house today, where it stays until April 23. Your speaking and writing abilities are strong now. You communicate effectively, especially related to your profession. Your ideas catch the interest of the public.

Tuesday, April 8 (Moon into Leo, 5:51 a.m.) Promote new ideas; follow your curiosity. Look for adventure. Freedom of thought and action is key. But so is moderation; avoid excess in whatever you're doing. You're motivated and inspired. You can overcome obstacles with ease.

Wednesday, April 9 (Moon in Leo) The moon is in your second house today. You could gain a financial boost that acts like a jolt of energy. You feel more secure. Decide your priorities in handling your finances. Even if you experience a sudden increase of income, put off any big purchases for a few days.

Thursday, April 10 (Moon into Virgo, 6:08 p.m.) It's a number 7 day. You're launching a journey into the unknown. Knowledge is essential to success. You're a spy for your own cause today. Go with the flow. Maintain your emotional balance, and don't make any absolute decisions until tomorrow.

Friday, April 11 (Moon in Virgo) The moon is in your third house. Your mental abilities are strong now, and you have an emotional need to reinvigorate your studies, especially regarding matters of the past. You could take an interest in history or archaeology. Relatives or neighbors play a role in your day. Stay in control of your emotions when dealing with them.

Saturday, April 12 (Moon in Virgo)   Under the influence of the Virgo moon, it's a good time to take care of details, especially related to a contract or partnership. Stop worrying and fretting. Dig deep for information. Take time to write in a journal. You write from a deep place with lots of details and colorful descriptions. Remember to exercise and watch your diet.

Sunday, April 13 (Moon into Libra, 4:34 a.m.) It's a number 1 day. Creativity is highlighted. Explore and discover. Get out and meet new people, have new experiences, do something you've never done before. In romance something new is brewing.

Monday, April 14 (Moon in Libra)   Pluto goes retrograde in your seventh house today, where it stays until September 22. You take a deeper look at a partnership, either personal or business. There could be some profound inner changes coming in your life.

Tuesday, April 15 (Moon into Scorpio, 12:21 p.m.) There's a lunar eclipse in your fourth house today. You have an emotional reaction to a development in your home. Children could play a role. With Mars forming a positive angle, whatever happens provides you with new energy and ultimately works to your advantage.

Wednesday, April 16 (Moon in Scorpio)   With the moon in your fifth house today, you're emotionally in touch with your creative side. In fact, your emotions tend to overpower your intellect. Be yourself; be emotionally honest. In love there's greater emotional depth to a relationship. You're more protective and nurturing toward children.

Thursday, April 17 (Moon into Sagittarius, 5:44 p.m.)   It's a number 5 day. Change and variety are highlighted. Think freedom, no restrictions. Release old structures; get a new point of view. It's a good day to take a risk, experiment. Promote new ideas. Find a new outlook that fits current circumstances and what you know now.

Friday, April 18 (Moon in Sagittarius)   The moon is in your sixth house today. It's a service day. Help others, but don't deny your own needs. It's a good day to clarify any health or work issues. It's best if you follow a regular schedule now.

Saturday, April 19 (Moon into Capricorn, 9:29 p.m.) Secrets, intrigue, confidential information play a role in your day. It could relate to a relationship, especially a romantic partner. Gather information, but don't make any absolute decisions until tomorrow. Go with the flow. Maintain your emotional balance. Avoid confusion and conflicts.

Sunday, April 20 (Moon in Capricorn)   The moon is in your seventh house today. The focus turns to relationships, business and personal ones. You get along well with others now. You comprehend the nuances of a situation, but it's difficult to go with the flow. Be careful that others don't manipulate your feelings.

Monday, April 21 (Moon in Capricorn) Under the influence of the Capricorn moon, your ambition and drive to succeed are highlighted. Self-discipline and structure are key. Your work load increases, and you might feel stressed and overworked. Don't ignore your exercise routine or your home life.

Tuesday, April 22 (Moon into Aquarius, 12:19 a.m.) It's a number 1 day. You're at the top of your cycle today. Take the lead; get a fresh start, a new beginning. Trust your hunches. In romance something new is developing. You're inventive and make connections that others overlook. You're determined and courageous. Stress originality.

Wednesday, April 23 (Moon in Aquarius) Mercury moves into your tenth house today. Your speaking and writing abilities flourish now. You communicate well with the public, and your efforts bolster your career. You gain recognition for what you do.

Thursday, April 24 (Moon into Pisces, 2:56 a.m.) It's a number 3 day. Your attitude determines everything today. Spread your good news, and take time to listen to others. Play your hunches and remain flexible. In romance you're an ardent and loyal lover.

Friday, April 25 (Moon in Pisces) The moon is in your ninth house today. You're a dreamer and a thinker. You may feel a need to get away now, a break from the usual routine. You yearn for a new experience. Plan a long trip. Sign up for a workshop or seminar. A foreigner or foreign country plays a role.

Saturday, April 26 (Moon into Aries, 6:02 a.m.)
It's a number 5 day. Change and variety are highlighted now. Promote new ideas; follow your curiosity. Approach the day with an unconventional mind-set. Let go of old structures; get a new point of view. Don't allow other people's moods to bring you down.

Sunday, April 27 (Moon in Aries)   The moon is in your tenth house today. Professional concerns are the focus of the day. You gain an elevation of prestige, possibly a raise or a promotion. You get along well with others in the workplace. Your life is more public now, so avoid emotional displays.

Monday, April 28 (Moon into Taurus, 10:24 a.m.)
It's a number 7 day. You work best on your own today. Secrets, intrigue, confidential information play a role. You investigate, analyze, or simply observe what's going on. You quickly come to a conclusion and wonder why others don't see what you see. You detect deception and recognize insincerity with ease. Maintain your emotional balance.

Tuesday, April 29 (Moon in Taurus)   There's a solar eclipse in your eleventh house today. That means new opportunities come your way related to friends and colleagues. Whatever is coming will benefit you, especially if you keep control of your emotions. With

Mercury forming a favorable angle, you communicate your ideas well, and they help you move ahead and take advantage of the opportunities.

Wednesday, April 30 (Moon into Gemini, 4:56 p.m.)
It's a number 9 day. Complete a project; clear up odds and ends. Take an inventory on where things are going in your life. Make room for something new, but don't start anything today.

MAY 2014

Thursday, May 1 (Moon in Gemini) The moon is in your twelfth house today. It's a good day to work behind the scenes and avoid any conflict. You could be dealing with a matter from the past that has returned to haunt you. Keep your feelings secret. Follow your intuition.

Friday, May 2 (Moon in Gemini) As Venus moves into your tenth house today, you're attracted to a creative project related to your career, especially something involving the arts or entertainment. You gain public attention or recognition. You're seen as appealing to the public.

Saturday, May 3 (Moon into Cancer, 2:13 a.m.)
It's a number 1 day. Your individuality is stressed. Take the initiative to start something new. You can turn in a new direction. Get out and meet new people; make new contacts. Make room for a new romance, if you're ready for it.

Sunday, May 4 (Moon in Cancer)   The moon is in your first house today. You're sensitive to other people's feelings. You may feel moody one moment, happy the next, then withdrawn and sad. It's all about your health and emotional self: how you feel and how you feel about yourself. You focus on how the public relates to you and how you can improve yourself.

Monday, May 5 (Moon into Leo, 1:56 p.m.)   Ease up on your routines, and spread your good news. You communicate well. You're warm and receptive to what others say. Your imagination is keen now. You're curious and inventive. Enjoy the harmony, beauty, and pleasures of life. Beautify your home.

Tuesday, May 6 (Moon in Leo)   With the moon in your second house, money issues surface. You could get a quick financial boost today. It's a good time for investments. Look at your priorities in spending your income. Take care of payments and collections. Alternately, self-worth issues come to light.

Wednesday, May 7 (Moon in Leo)   Mercury moves into your twelfth house today. Subconscious influences affect your thinking and play an important role in your day. You're secretive about your thoughts and ideas and more reserved than normal. You've got a lot on your mind now, but you tend to avoid speaking about it.

Thursday, May 8 (Moon into Virgo, 2:25 a.m.)   It's a number 6 day. Domestic purchases are highlighted. Focus on making people happy; do a good deed. It's a service day, so direct your energy toward helping others, Cancer. Be generous and tolerant, even if it goes against your nature.

Friday, May 9 (Moon in Virgo)   The moon is in your third house today. Your mental abilities are strong now, and you have an emotional need to reinvigorate your studies, especially regarding matters of the past. You also could be getting involved in a challenging mental activity, such as on-line gaming, a debate, or a game of chess. Take what you know and share it with others.

Saturday, May 10 (Moon into Libra, 1:20 p.m.) It's a number 8 day, your power day. You get an opportunity to expand and grow. Be courageous. You're playing with power, so be careful not to hurt others. Be aware that others in power may be watching your moves.

Sunday, May 11 (Moon in Libra)   The moon is in your fourth house. You're dealing with your home life and foundations. Spend time at home with family and loved ones. It's a good day to beautify your home or take care of minor repairs. Take time for meditation. See if you can remember your dreams from last night.

Monday, May 12 (Moon into Scorpio, 9:08 p.m.) It's a number 1 day, and you're at the top of your cycle again. Get out and meet new people, have new experiences, do something you've never done before. You're inventive and make connections that others overlook. You get a fresh start now. Trust your hunches.

Tuesday, May 13 (Moon in Scorpio)   The moon is in your fifth house today. Your love life takes off now. There's an idealistic turn to whatever you do for pleasure. It's a great time for a creative project, especially fiction writing. You could be somewhat possessive of loved ones and children. It's a good day to get a pet!

Wednesday, May 14 (Moon in Scorpio)   There's a full moon in your fifth house today. That means yesterday's energy flows into your Wednesday. Now you can reap what you've sown related to an artistic or creative project. With Saturn closely conjunct, you might be somewhat possessive of loved ones, particularly children. But eventually you need to let go.

Thursday, May 15 (Moon into Sagittarius, 1:45 a.m.)   It's a number 4 day. Hard work is called for. Persevere to get things done, and don't get sloppy. You're building a creative base. Control your impulses. Stay on course, and emphasize quality. It's not a good day for pursuing a romance.

Friday, May 16 (Moon in Sagittarius)   With the moon in your sixth house today, the emphasis turns to your daily work and service to others. Attend to all the details, Cancer. Be careful not to overlook any seemingly minor matters that could take on importance. Keep up with your exercise plan, and watch your diet.

Saturday, May 17 (Moon into Capricorn, 4:13 a.m.) You offer advice and support. Be sympathetic and kind, generous and tolerant. Focus on making people happy. Diplomacy wins the way. Be understanding, and avoid confrontations. Dance to your own tune.

Sunday, May 18 (Moon in Capricorn)   The moon is in your seventh house. The focus turns to relationships, business and personal ones. You get along well with others now. You can fit in just about anywhere, Cancer. But you're touchy and tend to avoid direct confrontations. You can also be somewhat manipulative.

Monday, May 19 (Moon into Aquarius, 5:59 a.m.) With Mars going direct in your fourth house today, Cancer, you tend to be more aggressive than usual related to a creative project or children. You forcefully push your point of view. You challenge others and can be somewhat combative in your position. Alternately, you could be aggressively dealing with a romantic partner.

Tuesday, May 20 (Moon in Aquarius)   The moon is in your eighth house today. You may attract power people to you. An interest in metaphysics could play a role. Your energy is more intense than usual. Your emotions could affect your feelings about belongings that you share with others.

Wednesday, May 21 (Moon into Pisces, 8:19 a.m.) It's a number 1 day, and you're at the top of your cycle. Be independent and creative and refuse to be discouraged by naysayers. Stress originality, and trust your hunches. You're determined and courageous today. In romance a flirtation turns more serious.

Thursday, May 22 (Moon in Pisces)   With the moon in your ninth house today, you're looking for something new. You may feel a need to get away now, a break from the usual routine. You're a dreamer and thinker. Higher education or long-distance travel plays a role.

Friday, May 23 (Moon into Aries, 12:02 p.m.) You're innovative and creative and communicate well. You can influence people now with your upbeat attitude. Your artistic talents are highlighted. Ease up on your routines, and spread your good news. Your charm and wit are appreciated. Remain flexible.

Saturday, May 24 (Moon in Aries)   With the moon in your tenth house today, professional concerns are highlighted. You gain a boost in prestige. You're warm and friendly toward coworkers. It's a good day for sales and dealing with the public.

Sunday, May 25 (Moon into Taurus, 5:28 p.m.) Change and variety are highlighted now. A change of scenery would work to your advantage. You could even be moving to a new location. Freedom of thought and action is key. But so is moderation; avoid excess in whatever you're doing.

Monday, May 26 (Moon in Taurus)   The moon is in your eleventh house today. You find meaning through friends and groups; there's strength in numbers. You work for the common good, but keep an eye on your own wishes and dreams. You work well with a group of like-minded individuals. At the same time you emphasize your individuality.

Tuesday, May 27 (Moon in Taurus)   Under the influence of the Taurus moon, your senses are highly attuned. You're opinionated and very sensual. Health and physical activity are highlighted. It's a good time for gardening, cultivating ideas, doing practical things. Try to avoid stubborn behavior.

Wednesday, May 28 (Moon into Gemini, 12:48 a.m.) With Venus moving into your eleventh house today, you love working with a group, especially on a project aimed at the common good. Alternately, you could be involved in a love relationship with a long-time friend or coworker. Meanwhile there's a new moon in your twelfth house, and that suggests new opportunities for creative work in solitude. With Uranus forming a beneficial angle, positive changes affect you deeply. A lover from the past could show up.

Thursday, May 29 (Moon in Gemini)   With Mercury moving into your first house, Cancer, you communicate extremely well. You also adapt quickly and smoothly to changing circumstances. Your mind is quick as you play with new ideas.

Friday, May 30 (Moon into Cancer, 10:14 a.m.) It's a number 1 day. You get a fresh start, a new beginning. Be independent and creative. Don't let others tell you what to do. Get out and meet new people, have new experiences, do something you've never done before. Express your opinions dynamically.

Saturday, May 31 (Moon in Cancer)   With the moon in your first house today, Cancer, you adapt easily to new situations. You're mentally fluid and look-ing for new ideas. You get batteries recharged for the month ahead. You're physically vital and get along well with the opposite sex.

JUNE 2014

Sunday, June 1 (Moon into Leo, 9:44 p.m.) It's a number 9 day. Visualize the future; set your goals, then make them so. Complete a project now; clear up odds and ends. Take an inventory on where things are going in your life. It's a good day to make a donation to a worthy cause.

Monday, June 2 (Moon in Leo) The moon is in your second house today. Money and material goods are important to you and give you a sense of security and self-worth, Cancer. You may be dealing with pay-ments and collecting what's owed to you. Look at your priorities in handling your income. Expect emo-tional experiences related to money or possibly your sense of self-worth.

Tuesday, June 3 (Moon in Leo) Under the influ-ence of the Leo moon, you're feeling bold and outgo-ing, especially related to matters in the workplace. You're creative and passionate. It's a good day to show off your new outfit, especially a sexy one! You're impulsive and honest, but try to avoid being a drama queen . . . or king.

Wednesday, June 4 (Moon into Virgo, 10:21 a.m.) Have fun today in preparation for tomorrow's discipline and focus. Take time to relax and recharge your batteries. Make time to listen to others. Your charm and wit are appreciated. Spread your good news; you communicate well.

Thursday, June 5 (Moon in Virgo)   The moon is in your third house today. You get your ideas across now, especially when you're talking to family members, siblings, and neighbors. But try not to get overly emotional, Cancer. You could be taking one or more short trips and possibly talking on your cell phone. Drive carefully, and take time to check up on your mother.

Friday, June 6 (Moon into Libra, 10:02 p.m.)   It's a number 5 day. Approach the day with an unconventional mindset. Release old structures; get a new point of view. Variety is the spice of life. Think freedom, no restrictions. Change and variety are highlighted now.

Saturday, June 7 (Moon in Libra)   Mercury goes retrograde in your first house today, where it stays until July 1. That means you can expect confusion or glitches related to your personal life, especially if you're dealing with an emotional or health issue. Others might misunderstand your shift of moods from happy to sad to joyous to withdrawn. You're searching for ways to improve yourself, but the changes you want seem to be taking forever.

Sunday, June 8 (Moon in Libra)   The moon is in your fourth house today. Spend time with your family and loved ones. Stick close to home, if possible. Take time to retreat to a private place for meditation. You're dealing with the foundations of who you are and who you are becoming. It's a good day for dream recall.

Monday, June 9 (Moon into Scorpio, 6:39 a.m.) Neptune goes retrograde in your ninth house today. You're getting intuitive nudges about delays in your plans for higher education or long-distance travel. Alternately, you could feel an urge to embrace a philosophy that is out of the ordinary, and that could cause some misunderstanding among friends, particularly someone born in a foreign land.

Tuesday, June 10 (Moon in Scorpio) With the moon in your fifth house today, it's a good day to take a chance, experiment. Be aware that your emotions tend to overpower your intellect now. You're emotionally in touch with your creative side. Alternately, you are more protective and nurturing toward children.

Wednesday, June 11 (Moon into Sagittarius, 11:24 a.m.) You're at the top of your cycle again, Cancer. Stress originality in whatever you're doing. Trust your hunches; intuition is highlighted. You're inventive and make connections that others overlook. You're determined and courageous today. A romantic partner could be entering your life, if you're looking for one.

Thursday, June 12 (Moon in Sagittarius) With the moon in your sixth house today, the emphasis turns to your daily work and service to others. Attend to all the details, Cancer. Be careful not to overlook any seemingly minor matters that could take on importance. Keep up with your exercise plan, and watch your diet.

Friday, June 13 (Moon into Capricorn, 1:05 p.m.)
There's a full moon in your sixth house today with Uranus forming a beneficial angle. That means you reap what you've sown related to your daily work or health. You gain insight regarding your efforts to help others in the workplace.

Saturday, June 14 (Moon in Capricorn) The moon is in your seventh house today. You get along well with others. You can fit in just about anywhere. Loved ones and partners are more important than usual. You comprehend the nuances of a situation, but it's difficult to go with the flow. Be careful that others don't manipulate your feelings.

Sunday, June 15 (Moon into Aquarius, 1:28 p.m.)
It's a number 5 day. Approach the day with an unconventional mindset. Release old structures; get a new point of view. Variety is the spice of life. Think freedom, no restrictions. Change and variety are highlighted now.

Monday, June 16 (Moon in Aquarius) The moon is in your eighth house today. You attract the attention of powerful people. Be aware that your experiences could be more intense than usual. You could be dealing with a matter related to shared belongings, investments, or taxes. An interest in metaphysics plays a role. You could be reading about concepts of life after death.

Tuesday, June 17 (Moon into Pisces, 2:26 p.m.)
It's a number 7 day. Secrets, intrigue, confidential information play a role. You investigate activities taking place behind closed doors—literally or figuratively. You work best on your own today. Keep your own counsel. Knowledge is essential to success. Gather information, but don't make any absolute decisions until tomorrow.

Wednesday, June 18 (Moon in Pisces) With the moon in your ninth house today, you may feel a need to get away, a break from the usual routine. You yearn for a new experience. Plan a long trip. Sign up for a workshop or seminar. Higher education and travel are emphasized.

Thursday, June 19 (Moon into Aries, 5:26 p.m.)
It's a great time for completing projects and getting ready for something new. Clear up odds and ends. Take an inventory on where things are going in your life. It's time to make a donation to a worthy cause. Look beyond the present.

Friday, June 20 (Moon in Aries) The moon is in your tenth house today. You're attracted to a creative project in your career, especially something involving the arts or entertainment. You gain public attention or recognition. You're feeling grounded and stable. You're also appealing to the public.

Saturday, June 21 (Moon into Taurus, 11:03 p.m.)
It's a number 2 day, and issues related to a relationship or partnership are highlighted. The spotlight is on cooperation now, but expect some soul-searching related to a relationship. New relationships form. Help comes through friends.

Sunday, June 22 (Moon in Taurus)   The moon is in your eleventh house today. You find strength in numbers and meaning through friends and groups. Your sense of security is tied to your relationships and friends. Focus on your wishes and dreams. Examine your overall goals. Those goals should be an expression of who you are.

Monday, June 23 (Moon in Taurus)   Venus moves into your twelfth house, suggesting that you'll feel best working out personal issues by remaining behind the scenes. Alternately, a lover from the past could re-emerge into your life. Avoid confrontations, and take time to meditate.

Tuesday, June 24 (Moon into Gemini, 7:06 a.m.)
It's a number 5 day. You're restless and looking for change, a new perspective. You're versatile and changeable, but be careful not to overcommit yourself now. Stay focused as best you can. Take risks, experiment. Pursue a new idea. Freedom of thought and action is key.

Wednesday, June 25 (Moon in Gemini)   The moon is in your twelfth house today. It's a good day to withdraw and spend time in private. Relax and meditate. Keep your feelings to yourself, and focus on making people happy. Service to others is the theme of the day. It's a great day for pursuing a mystical or spiritual discipline.

Thursday, June 26 (Moon into Cancer, 5:06 p.m.) You investigate, analyze, or simply observe what's going on now. You quickly come to a conclusion and wonder why others don't see what you see. You detect deception and recognize insincerity with ease, but don't make any absolute decisions until tomorrow.

Friday, June 27 (Moon in Cancer)   There's a new moon in your first house today. Look for new opportunities related to your willingness to change and adjust to new circumstances. You're recharged for the month ahead, and you have a chance to appear more in front of the public.

Saturday, June 28 (Moon in Cancer)   Under the influence of the Cancer moon, you're emotionally attached to your home now. You can focus with ease today on an artistic endeavor in the home. Snuggle with a loved one. You're sensitive to other people's moods.

Sunday, June 29 (Moon into Leo, 4:44 a.m.)   It's a number 1 day, and you're at the top of your cycle again. You get a fresh start. Creativity is emphasized, and don't be afraid to turn in a new direction. Get out and meet new people. In romance something new is developing.

Monday, June 30 (Moon in Leo)   The moon is in your second house today. Money and material goods are important to you now and give you a sense of security. You identify emotionally with your possessions or whatever you value. Watch your spending.

JULY 2014

Tuesday, July 1 (Moon into Virgo, 5:25 p.m.)   Mercury moves into your twelfth house today. Your unconscious mind strongly influences your thoughts and actions. Matters from the past arise, and you confide in a friend. Emotions, rather than logic, dictate your decisions.

Wednesday, July 2 (Moon in Virgo)   The moon is in your third house today. You get your ideas across now, Cancer, especially when you're talking to family members, siblings, and neighbors. You could be taking one or more short trips and possibly talking on your cell phone. Drive carefully, and take time to check up on your mother.

Thursday, July 3 (Moon in Virgo)   Under the influence of the Virgo moon, it's a good time to take care of details, especially related to a contract or partnership. Stop worrying and fretting. Dig deep for information. Take time to write in a journal. You write from a deep place with lots of details and colorful descriptions. Remember to exercise and watch your diet.

Friday, July 4 (Moon into Libra, 5:44 a.m.)   It's a number 4 day. It's a good day to get organized. Clean out your garage, attic, or a closet. Tear down the old in order to rebuild. Be methodical and thorough. Missing papers are found. Revise and rewrite. You're building a creative base. Happy Independence Day.

Saturday, July 5 (Moon in Libra)   The moon is in your fifth house today. You're emotionally in touch with your creative side as your emotions overpower your intellect. In love there's greater emotional depth to a relationship. Be yourself; be emotionally honest.

Sunday, July 6 (Moon into Scorpio, 3:34 p.m.)   It's time to make an adjustment in your home life. You could face emotional outbursts or someone making unfair demands, but everything works out. Be understanding, and avoid confrontations. Offer advice and support, but do it in a diplomatic way.

Monday, July 7 (Moon in Scorpio)   Under the influence of the Scorpio moon, your emotions grow intense as you investigate an important matter. Control issues arise. Be aware of things happening in secret. Forgive and forget; try to avoid going to extremes. You're also passionate today, and your sexuality is heightened.

Tuesday, July 8 (Moon into Sagittarius, 9:25 p.m.) It's a number 8 day, your power day. So focus on a power play. You can go far with your plans and achieve financial success. Open your mind to a new approach that could bring in big bucks. It's a good day to buy a lotto ticket.

Wednesday, July 9 (Moon in Sagittarius)   With the moon in your sixth house today, the emphasis turns to your daily work, health, and service to others. Look for ways to expand, Cancer. Be careful not to overlook any seemingly minor matters that could take on importance. Keep up with your exercise plan, and watch your diet.

Thursday, July 10 (Moon into Capricorn, 11:25 p.m.)   You're determined and courageous today. Stress originality in whatever you're doing. Be independent and creative, and don't be afraid to turn in a new direction. Refuse to deal with people who have closed minds. Explore, discover, create. In romance something new could be brewing. A flirtation turns more serious.

Friday, July 11 (Moon in Capricorn)   With the moon in your seventh house today, the emphasis is on partnerships, marriage, and contracts. Women play a prominent role in your day. You get along well with others now. You can fit in just about anywhere. Just be careful that no one manipulates your feelings.

Saturday, July 12 (Moon into Aquarius, 11:07 p.m.)   Mercury is still direct in your first house today. That means you tell others about personal issues that are bothering you. Your mind is especially quick, and you make your point clearly. There's also a full moon in your seventh house, indicating that you reap what you've sown related to a partnership, either personal or business related.

Sunday, July 13 (Moon in Aquarius) The moon is in your eighth house today. You attract the attention of powerful people. You could be dealing with a matter related to shared belongings, investments, or taxes. An interest in metaphysics plays a role. You could be studying or discussing ideas about life after death or reincarnation. Be aware that your experiences could be more intense than usual.

Monday, July 14 (Moon into Pisces, 10:41 p.m.) It's a number 5 day. Release old structures; get a new point of view. Change your perspective. Approach the day with an unconventional mindset. Think outside the box; look for variety rather than the same old thing.

Tuesday, July 15 (Moon in Pisces) The moon is in your ninth house today, the home of higher learning. You're full of ideas now on matters such as philosophy or religion, the law or publishing. You also have a strong interest in foreign travel or a foreign nation. It's a good time to look to the big picture. Break away from your routine or the usual way you think about things.

Wednesday, July 16 (Moon in Pisces) Jupiter moves into your second house today. Over the coming weeks and months you have a good chance of expanding your income and bolstering your finances. You might increase your sense of self-worth by whatever it is that develops. Be aware that you need to remain flexible and versatile.

Thursday, July 17 (Moon into Aries, 12:07 a.m.)
It's a number 8 day, your power day, Cancer. You attract financial success. You can go far with your plans, especially if you open your mind to a new approach. Be aware that you're playing with power, so try not to hurt anyone.

Friday, July 18 (Moon in Aries)   Venus moves into your first house today. You're friendly and outgoing, moving from one group of friends or associates to another. Your charm and wit are appreciated. Your attitude determines everything. Your vitality is strong, and you have a natural ability to express yourself.

Saturday, July 19 (Moon into Taurus, 4:43 a.m.)
It's a number 1 day, and you're at the top of your cycle. Take the initiative to start something new. Individuality is stressed. You can turn in a new direction. Get out and meet new people; make new contacts. Make room for a new romance, if you're ready for it.

Sunday, July 20 (Moon in Taurus)   Saturn goes direct in your fifth house today. You're moving into a period of greater mental discipline and more structure to your work life, especially related to your creative projects. The emphasis is on pursuing practical options and not taking chances. You could encounter some feelings of depression. Be particularly cautious in getting involved romantically with someone in the office.

Monday, July 21 (Moon into Gemini, 12:37 p.m.)
Uranus goes retrograde in your tenth house, and that

could mean some erratic and unexpected developments related to your career. Try to avoid making mountains out of molehills. You may be looking deeply into your professional life, reconsidering your direction or goals and wondering how past events are affecting you. You could experience bursts of intuitive energy related to your interest in gaining more recognition or status.

Tuesday, July 22 (Moon in Gemini)   The moon is in your twelfth house today. Best to work behind the scenes and avoid any conflicts and confrontations, especially with women. Keep your feelings secret. Unconscious attitudes can be difficult.

Wednesday, July 23 (Moon into Cancer, 11:00 p.m.) It's a number 5 day, and that means you have a greater sense of freedom. Release old structures; get a new point of view. You're versatile and changeable. Think outside the box. Take risks, experiment.

Thursday, July 24 (Moon in Cancer)   The moon is in your first house today. Best to work behind the scenes and avoid any conflicts and confrontations, especially with women. Keep your feelings secret. Unconscious attitudes can be difficult.

Friday, July 25 (Moon in Cancer)   Mars moves into your fifth house today, suggesting that you're aggressively dealing with matters related to a romantic relationship or creative project. Children play a role, and sports could be involved.

Saturday, July 26 (Moon into Leo, 10:56 a.m.)
There's a new moon in your second house today, and
Jupiter is closely conjunct. Watch for new opportunities to increase your income; you have a chance to
expand into new areas. You see the big picture.

Sunday, July 27 (Moon in Leo)   The moon is in
your second house today. You could be feeling quite
magnanimous and impulsive now, especially related
to finances. Your generosity is appreciated. However,
watch your spending. You feel best in the home setting, surrounded by family, friends, and familiar objects.

Monday, July 28 (Moon into Virgo, 11:37 p.m.)
You're at the top of your cycle again. Be independent
and creative and refuse to be discouraged by naysayers. Stress originality, and trust your hunches. You're
determined and courageous today. In romance a flirtation turns more serious.

Tuesday, July 29 (Moon in Virgo)   The moon is in
your third house today. Your mental abilities are
strong, and you have an emotional need to investigate
matters related to the past. Take what you know, and
share it with others. You get your ideas across, but try
not to get too emotional. A female relative plays an
important role.

Wednesday, July 30 (Moon in Virgo)   Under the
influence of the Virgo moon, you may exhibit some
perfectionist tendencies. Take care of details now, especially related to your health. Exercise, and watch

your diet. Stop worrying and fretting. Take time to write in a journal. You write from a deep place with lots of details and colorful descriptions.

Thursday, July 31 (Moon into Libra, 12:10 p.m.)
It's a number 4 day. Persevere to get things done today. Don't get sloppy. Do things like clean your closet, clear your desk, straighten up your garage. Tear down the old in order to rebuild. Be methodical and thorough. You could be preparing for a long journey or a pursuit of higher education.

AUGUST 2014

Friday, August 1 (Moon in Libra)   The moon is in your fourth house. You're dealing with your home life and the foundations of who you are. Spend time at home with family and loved ones, Cancer, a comfortable place for you. Take the day off, if possible, or work at home. It's a good day to handle domestic repairs. Spend some time in meditation.

Saturday, August 2 (Moon into Scorpio, 10:57 p.m.)
It's a number 3 day. Ease up on your routines, and spread your good news. You communicate well. You're warm and receptive to what others say. Your imagination is keen now. You're curious and inventive. Enjoy the harmony, beauty, and pleasures of life.

Sunday, August 3 (Moon in Scorpio)   The moon is in your fifth house today. Your love life takes off. There's an idealistic turn to whatever you do for pleasure. It's a great time for a creative project, especially fiction writing. You could be somewhat posses-sive of loved ones and children. It's a good day to get a pet!

Monday, August 4 (Moon in Scorpio)   Under the influence of the Scorpio moon, yesterday's energy flows into your Monday. Your emotions grow intense as you investigate an important matter. Control issues arise. Be aware of things happening in secret. Forgive and forget; try to avoid going to extremes. You're also passionate today, and your sexuality is heightened.

Tuesday, August 5 (Moon into Sagittarius, 6:19 a.m.) It's a number 6 day. Service to others is the theme of the day. Focus on making people happy. You offer ad-vice and support. Be diplomatic rather than confron-tational. Try to keep everyone around you in balance. Do a good deed for someone.

Wednesday, August 6 (Moon in Sagittarius)   With the moon in your sixth house today, the emphasis turns to your daily work and service to others. Attend to all the details, Cancer. Be careful not to overlook any seemingly minor matters that could take on im-portance. Keep up with your exercise plan, and watch your diet.

Thursday, August 7 (Moon into Capricorn, 9:39 a.m.)   You get an opportunity to expand and grow today. Be courageous. You're playing with power, so be careful not to hurt others. Be aware that those in power may be watching your moves.

Friday, August 8 (Moon in Capricorn)　The moon is in your seventh house today. You could be negotiating or signing a contract now, possibly for the sale of your house. You're taking the initiative with your partner, and emotions could get volatile. It's difficult to maintain an objective and detached point of view. Be careful not to let others manipulate your feelings.

Saturday, August 9 (Moon into Aquarius, 9:53 a.m.) It's a number 1 day, and you're at the top of your cycle. Be independent and creative; consider turning in a new direction. You get a fresh start now. Trust your hunches. In romance something new is developing.

Sunday, August 10 (Moon in Aquarius)　There's a full moon in your eighth house today. Matters about shared income or possessions come to a head. You are provoking change, and your partner is finally listening to you. With Uranus forming a beneficial angle, you gain sudden insight related to a metaphysical topic, such as life after death. You could be inspired to get a reading from a medium.

Monday, August 11 (Moon into Pisces, 8:56 a.m.) Ease up on your routines, and spread your good news. You communicate well. You're warm and receptive to what others say. Your imagination is keen; you're curious and inventive. Enjoy the harmony, beauty, and pleasures of life. Beautify your home.

Tuesday, August 12 (Moon in Pisces)　With Venus in your second house, you love personal adornments and enjoy showing them off. It's a good time for making money. You feel good now about the status that financial success brings you, especially if you achieve your success through your art or creative endeavors.

Wednesday, August 13 (Moon into Aries, 9:01 a.m.)
You're restless and looking for change, a new perspective. You're versatile and changeable, but be careful not to overcommit yourself now. Stay focused as best you can. Take risks, experiment; pursue a new idea. Freedom of thought and action is key.

Thursday, August 14 (Moon in Aries)   With the moon in your tenth house, you end the week focused on your professional life. You gain a boost in prestige, possibly a raise. You get along well with coworkers. Your life is more in public view. Your hard work is appreciated, Cancer.

Friday, August 15 (Moon into Taurus, 11:59 a.m.)
Mercury moves into your third house today. There's lots of mental activity related to your everyday life. Siblings, other relatives, or neighbors play a role. It could also mean that things are changing in the way you communicate, and you need to make adjustments.

Saturday, August 16 (Moon in Taurus)   The moon is in your eleventh house. Friends play an important role in your day, and you take the initiative to get together with them. You find strength in numbers and meaning through friends and groups. Libra and Aquarius friends fit well with you now.

Sunday, August 17 (Moon into Gemini, 6:42 p.m.)
It's a number 9 day. It's time to complete a project.
Clear your desk, and make room for the new, but
don't start anything until tomorrow. Spend some time
in deep thought. Consider how you can expand your
base. Strive for universal appeal.

Monday, August 18 (Moon in Gemini) The
moon is in your twelfth house today. Think carefully
before you act. There's a tendency now to undo all the
positive actions you've taken. Avoid any self-
destructive behavior. It's best to work behind the
scenes and stay out of the public view. Be aware of
hidden enemies.

Tuesday, August 19 (Moon in Gemini) Under
the influence of the Gemini moon, you're mentally
quick and communicate well. You see two sides of an
issue. You're feeling creative and need to express
yourself in writing. A change of scenery would do you
good today, possibly a short trip to visit friends or
relatives.

*Wednesday, August 20 (Moon into Cancer, 4:46
a.m.)* Take time to beautify your home, Cancer.
Enjoy the harmony, beauty, and pleasures of life. Remain flexible. Your imagination is keen; you're curious
and inventive. You communicate well today. You're
warm and receptive to what others say.

Thursday, August 21 (Moon in Cancer) The
moon is in your first house today. You are sensitive
and responsive regarding the needs of others. But

you're restless and somewhat uncertain what to do. Your self-awareness and appearance are important now. It's all about your health and emotional self: how you feel and how you feel about yourself.

Friday, August 22 (Moon into Leo, 4:50 p.m.) It's a number 5 day. You're restless and looking for change, a new perspective. You're versatile and changeable, but be careful not to overcommit yourself now. Stay focused as best you can. Take risks, experiment. Pursue a new idea. Freedom of thought and action is key.

Saturday, August 23 (Moon in Leo) The moon is in your second house. That means you could gain a financial boost that feels like a jolt of energy. Money and material goods are important to you now and give you a sense of security.

Sunday, August 24 (Moon in Leo) Under the influence of the Leo moon, you're at center stage now, Cancer. Dress boldly. Showmanship is highlighted, so are romance and love. Be wild, imaginative; be the person you always imagined you might be. Play with different personae.

Monday, August 25 (Moon into Virgo, 5:33 a.m.) New opportunities come your way now, Cancer, especially related to your ability to communicate. It's a good time to begin a new project. Relatives, especially siblings, contact you and could be surprisingly helpful. Avoid getting overly emotional or bombastic, though, when you express your point of view.

Tuesday, August 26 (Moon in Virgo)   Under the influence of the Virgo moon, you could exhibit some perfectionist tendencies. Take care of details, especially related to your health. Exercise; watch your diet. You respond emotionally to whatever is happening now, Cancer. But stop worrying and fretting.

Wednesday, August 27 (Moon into Libra, 5:54 p.m.) You get a fresh start now, a new beginning. Get out and meet new people, have new experiences, do something you've never done before. You're inventive and make connections that others overlook. Trust your hunches.

Thursday, August 28 (Moon in Libra)   Under the influence of the Libra moon, romance is highlighted. Relationship issues figure prominently in your day. It's a great day to schedule an adventurous encounter with your significant other. You're also looking for balance as you fine-tune a love relationship. Compassion is highlighted.

Friday, August 29 (Moon in Libra)   The moon is in your fourth house today, your native home, Cancer. You're dealing with your domestic life and the foundations of who you are. Spend time at home with family and loved ones. Take the day off, if possible, or work at home. It's a good day to handle repairs on your house. Spend some time in meditation.

Saturday, August 30 (Moon into Scorpio, 4:53 a.m.) It's a number 4 day. That means the emphasis today is on your organizational skills. In romance your per-

sistence pays off, Cancer. You're building a foundation for the future. Control your impulse to wander;
fulfill your obligations. You could find missing papers
now.

Sunday, August 31 (Moon in Scorpio)   The moon
is in your fifth house today. Your love life takes off
now. There's an idealistic turn to whatever you do for
pleasure, Cancer. It's a great time for pursuing an artistic or creative project. You could be somewhat sensitive and possessive of loved ones and children. It's a
good day to get a pet!

SEPTEMBER 2014

**Monday, September 1 (Moon into Sagittarius, 1:17
p.m.)**   Ease up on your routines, and spread your
good news. You communicate well. You're warm and
receptive to what others say. Your imagination is keen;
you're curious and inventive. Enjoy the harmony,
beauty, and pleasures of life. Beautify your home.

Tuesday, September 2 (Moon in Sagittarius)   Mercury moves into your fourth house today. There's lots
of mental activity in the home now. Home schooling
or games requiring mental skills are a possibility at
this time. It could also mean that things are changing
in the home, and you need to make adjustments.

**Wednesday, September 3 (Moon into Capricorn, 6:16
p.m.)**   You're seeking new horizons. Think outside
the box. Approach the day with an unconventional
mindset. Take risks, experiment. Travel and variety are

highlighted today. You're also more comfortable than usual in front of an audience

Thursday, September 4 (Moon in Capricorn) With the moon in your seventh house today, the emphasis is on partnerships, marriage and contracts. Women play a prominent role in your day. You get along well with others. You can fit in just about anywhere. Just be careful that no one manipulates your feelings.

Friday, September 5 (Moon into Aquarius, 8:00 p.m.) You investigate, analyze, or simply observe what's going on now. You quickly come to a conclusion and wonder why others don't see what you see. You detect deception and recognize insincerity with ease.

Saturday, September 6 (Moon in Aquarius) Under the influence of the Aquarius moon, your individuality is stressed. You might feel like remaining behind the scenes, but be aware that help is available through friends. Your visionary abilities are heightened. Play your hunches. Look beyond the immediate; bust old paradigms.

Sunday, September 7 (Moon into Pisces, 7:48 p.m.) It's time to complete a project. Clear your desk, and make room for the new, but don't start anything until tomorrow. Spend some time in deep thought. Consider how you can expand your base. Strive for universal appeal.

Monday, September 8 (Moon in Pisces) There's a full moon in your ninth house today. You reap what you've sown regarding higher education or long-distance travel. Your mind is active, and you yearn for new experiences, a break from the routine, a change from the status quo. With Saturn forming a beneficial angle, whatever you hear about is a serious matter. Saturn also brings more structure into your life and allows you to take advantage of what you've learned.

Tuesday, September 9 (Moon into Aries, 7:34 p.m.) Cooperation and partnerships are highlighted. You're diplomatic and capable of fixing whatever has gone wrong. You're concerned about keeping everything in balance, Cancer. You excel in working with a group. You're playing the role of the visionary today. Be honest and open.

Wednesday, September 10 (Moon in Aries) With the moon in your tenth house today, it's a good day for sales and dealing with the public. You get a boost in prestige. You get along with fellow workers, and you're sensitive to their needs.

Thursday, September 11 (Moon into Taurus, 9:17 p.m.) It's a number 4 day. Persevere to get things done today. Don't get sloppy. Do things like clearing your desk, cleaning a closet, or straightening up your garage. Tear down the old in order to rebuild. Be methodical and thorough. You could be preparing for a long journey or a pursuit of higher education.

Friday, September 12 (Moon in Taurus) Yesterday's energy flows into your Friday. You find strength in numbers. You find meaning through friends and groups. Social consciousness plays a role. You work for the common good, but again keep an eye on your own wishes and dreams.

Saturday, September 13 (Moon in Taurus)   Mars moves into your sixth house today. There's a lot going on at work now. Even though you'll be very busy this fall, take care of your health. Take time to exercise, and look for a new nutrition program.

Sunday, September 14 (Moon into Gemini, 2:27 a.m.)   You journey into the unknown today and investigate something hidden that's going on behind the scenes. You dig deep as you explore a mystery. Knowledge is essential to your success.

Monday, September 15 (Moon in Gemini)   The moon is in your twelfth house today. Think carefully before you act. There's a tendency now to undo all the positive actions you've taken. Avoid any self-destructive behavior. It's best to work behind the scenes and stay out of the public view. Be aware of hidden enemies.

Tuesday, September 16 (Moon into Cancer, 11:24 a.m.)   It's a number 9 day. Finish what you started. Visualize the future; set your goals, then make them so. Look beyond the immediate. Get ready for something new. Strive for universal appeal.

Wednesday, September 17 (Moon in Cancer)   The moon is in your first house today. Your batteries are recharged for the month ahead. You're more appealing to the public. Relations with the opposite sex go well. Your feelings and thoughts are aligned.

Thursday, September 18 (Moon into Leo, 11:10 p.m.) You're nurturing and contemplative today. Don't make waves; don't rush or show resentment. Let things develop. Cooperation is highlighted. So is your intuition. Be kind and understanding.

Friday, September 19 (Moon in Leo) The moon is in your second house, Cancer, indicating that you can come up with some money-making ideas this month. Your mind is focused on financial affairs, and you can easily communicate your thoughts so that your ideas can be put into place. Your values now deal primarily with material success.

Saturday, September 20 (Moon in Leo) Yesterday's energy flows into your Saturday. You tend to equate your financial assets with emotional security. Look at your priorities in handling any new income. Put off making any major purchases now. Your sense of self-worth plays a role.

Sunday, September 21 (Moon into Virgo, 11:54 a.m.) You're versatile and changeable, Cancer. Be careful not to spread out and diversify too much. Promote new ideas; follow your curiosity. Look for adventure. Freedom of thought and action is key. But so is moderation; avoid excess in whatever you're doing.

Monday, September 22 (Moon in Virgo) Pluto goes direct in your seventh house today. You feel very attached to your ideas about partnerships. You'll stay with these concepts for years. At the same time there could be some tension with those around you over the way you think about relationships or how you deal with legal matters. Be aware of any power struggles, and see if you can diffuse them before they get out of control.

Tuesday, September 23 (Moon in Virgo) The moon is in your third house today. You write from a deep place. It's a good day for journaling or working on any writing project. Your thinking now could be heavily influenced by matters from the past. A female relative plays a role.

Wednesday, September 24 (Moon into Libra, midnight) There's a new moon in your fourth house today, and that means new opportunities come your way related to working in your home. You might begin a new home-based business aimed at helping others. With Mars forming a beneficial angle, you can aggressively move ahead with your plans.

Thursday, September 25 (Moon in Libra) The moon is in your fourth house today. Spend time with your family and loved ones. Stick close to home, if possible. You're dealing with the foundations of who you are and who you are becoming. It's a good day to work on a home-repair project. Or you might buy something to beauty your environment.

Friday, September 26 (Moon into Scorpio, 10:30 a.m.) It's a number 1 day, Cancer, and you're at the top of your cycle. Be independent and creative, and refuse to be discouraged by naysayers. Trust your hunches; intuition is highlighted. It's time for a fresh start, and don't be afraid to turn in a new direction.

Saturday, September 27 (Moon in Scorpio)   Mercury moves into your fifth house today. You express yourself well and forcefully, both in writing and speaking. You are understood, and people pay attention to what you say. In romance you tend to be analytical now, weighing all sides of a relationship. Try not to be overly critical with your mate.

Sunday, September 28 (Moon into Sagittarius, 6:51 p.m.)   It's a number 3 day. Take time to relax, enjoy yourself, recharge your batteries. You can influence people now with your upbeat attitude, Cancer. Your charm and wit are appreciated. Foster generosity. In romance you're an ardent and loyal lover.

Monday, September 29 (Moon in Sagittarius) The moon is in your sixth house today. Working at home now is enjoyable and pays off. Spend more time at home with loved ones. Beautify your surroundings with a repair or redecoration project. Show that you care. It's also a good day to retreat to a private place for meditation and put everything into perspective.

Tuesday, September 30 (Moon in Sagittarius) With the moon in your sixth house today, the emphasis turns to your daily work and service to others. Attend to all the details, Cancer. Be careful not to overlook any seemingly minor matters that could take on importance. You're sensitive and can be somewhat defensive. Keep up with your exercise plan, and watch your diet.

OCTOBER 2014

Wednesday, October 1 (Moon into Capricorn, 12:42 a.m.) It's a number 4 day. Your organizational skills are highlighted. Control your impulses. Set aside romantic notions for the time being. Persevere and fulfill your obligations. You're building foundations for your creativity. Emphasize quality.

Thursday, October 2 (Moon in Capricorn) The moon is in your seventh house today as the focus turns to partnerships, both personal and business. A legal matter could be involved. Women play a prominent role. You get along well with others now, but be careful that they don't manipulate your feelings.

Friday, October 3 (Moon into Aquarius, 4:01 a.m.) It's a number 6 day. Focus on making people happy today. You offer advice and support. Visit someone who is ill or in need of help. A domestic adjustment works out for the best. Be understanding, and avoid confrontations.

Saturday, October 4 (Moon in Aquarius) Mercury goes retrograde in your fifth house, where it stays until October 25. That means you can expect some delays, misunderstandings, and miscommunication over the next three weeks, especially related to a romance or creative project. Relax, and control your emotional reaction to situations.

Sunday, October 5 (Moon into Pisces, 5:25 a.m.)
It's your power day. Unexpected money comes your way. You attract financial success. Be courageous. Be yourself; be honest. Appear successful now, even if you don't feel that way.

Monday, October 6 (Moon in Pisces) The moon is in your ninth house today, the home of higher learning. You're full of ideas now on matters such as philosophy or religion, the law or publishing. You also have a strong interest in foreign travel or a foreign nation. It's a good time to look to the big picture, Cancer. Break away from your routine or the usual way you think about things.

Tuesday, October 7 (Moon into Aries, 6:07 a.m.)
It's a number 1 day, so you're at the top of your cycle. It's a great time for initiating new projects, launching new ideas, or brainstorming for new ways of making money. You take the lead on something new as you get a fresh start. Follow your heart.

Wednesday, October 8 (Moon in Aries) There's a lunar eclipse in your tenth house today. That means you have an emotional reaction to an event that relates to your career. With Uranus forming a close angle, whatever this event is comes suddenly and without warning. You're more open and accessible now, but take care to avoid emotional displays, especially in public.

Thursday, October 9 (Moon into Taurus, 7:44 a.m.)
It's a number 3 day. You come out of your shell. You communicate well. You're warm and receptive to

what others say. Spread your good news. Ease up on routines. Your charm and wit are appreciated. Play your hunches.

Friday, October 10 (Moon in Taurus)   The moon is in your eleventh house today. You find strength in numbers. You find meaning through friends and groups. Your sense of security is tied to your relationships and to your friends.

Saturday, October 11 (Moon into Gemini, 11:51 a.m.)   It's a number 5 day. Approach the day with an unconventional mindset. Let go of old structures; get a new point of view. Think freedom, no restrictions. Change and variety are highlighted now. It's a good time to experiment.

Sunday, October 12 (Moon in Gemini)   The moon is in your twelfth house today. You might feel a need to withdraw and work behind the scenes. Matters from the past, possibly your childhood, play a role. It's best to hide your emotions and moodiness. But you might confide in a true friend.

Monday, October 13 (Moon into Cancer, 7:31 p.m.) You investigate, analyze, or simply observe what's going on now. You quickly come to a conclusion and wonder why others don't see what you see. You detect deception and recognize insincerity with ease, but don't make any absolute decisions until tomorrow.

Tuesday, October 14 (Moon in Cancer)   With the moon in your first house today, you're riding on a new wave, Cancer, and getting recharged for the rest of the month. Your thoughts and emotions are aligned. You could be somewhat moody, shifting from happy one moment, sad the next, then back again. You're dealing with your self-awareness, your appearance, and the person you are becoming.

Wednesday, October 15 (Moon in Cancer)   You're physically vital, and relations with the opposite sex go well. It's a good time to plan a long trip or sign up for a workshop or seminar. Worldviews are emphasized. Your appearance and personality shine.

Thursday, October 16 (Moon into Leo, 6:30 a.m.) It's a number 1 day, and you're at the top of your cycle again. You're determined and courageous today. Stress originality in whatever you're doing. Refuse to deal with people who have closed minds. Explore, discover, create. In romance something new could be brewing. A flirtation turns more serious.

Friday, October 17 (Moon in Leo)   The moon is in your second house today. Money and material goods are important to you now and give you a sense of security. You identify emotionally with your possessions or whatever you value. Watch your spending.

Saturday, October 18 (Moon into Virgo, 7:09 p.m.) You're warm and receptive to what others say. Your imagination is keen; you're curious and inventive. Enjoy the harmony, beauty, and pleasures of life. You have a strong sense of duty and feel obligated to fulfill your promises.

Sunday, October 19 (Moon in Virgo)   The moon is in your third house today. You get your ideas across now, Cancer, especially when you're talking to family members, siblings, and neighbors. You could be taking one or more short trips and possibly talking on your cell phone. Drive carefully, and take time to check up on your mother.

Monday, October 20 (Moon in Virgo)   Under the influence of the Virgo moon, it's a good time to take care of details, especially related to a contract or partnership. Stop worrying and fretting. Dig deep for information. Spell it all out in a journal. Remember to exercise and watch your diet.

Tuesday, October 21 (Moon into Libra, 7:13 a.m.)
It's a number 6 day. A domestic adjustment works out for the best. You could face emotional outbursts or someone making unfair demands. Be understanding, and avoid confrontations. Offer advice and support, but do it in a diplomatic way.

Wednesday, October 22 (Moon in Libra)   The moon is in your fourth house today. Spend time with your family and loved ones. Stick close to home if possible. You feel a close tie to your roots. You're dealing with the foundations of who you are and who you are becoming. A parent plays a role.

Thursday, October 23 (Moon into Scorpio, 5:11 p.m.)   Venus moves into your fifth house today, and there's also a new moon in Scorpio. Opportunities for creative projects abound, especially in your home.

Alternately, you could find yourself in the midst of a torrid relationship. Feelings are heightened, and passions run high.

Friday, October 24 (Moon in Scorpio)   The moon is in your fifth house today. Your emotions tend to overpower your intellect as yesterday's energy flows into your Friday. Be yourself; be emotionally honest. In love there's greater emotional depth to a relationship now. Creativity is emphasized.

Saturday, October 25 (Moon in Scorpio)   Mercury goes direct in your fourth house today. Confusion, miscommunication, and delays, especially related to your home life, recede into the past. Things move more smoothly. You get your message across. Everything works better, including computers and other electronic equipment. Misunderstandings about a health issue are resolved.

Sunday, October 26 (Moon into Sagittarius, 12:41 a.m.)   Mars moves into your seventh house today, providing energy for partnerships. A legal matter comes to your attention, and you move aggressively to deal with it over the next few weeks. It's also a good time to take a risk.

Monday, October 27 (Moon in Sagittarius)   The moon is in your sixth house today. Your personal health occupies your attention now. Keep your resolutions about exercise, and watch your diet. Attend to details related to your making a doctor or dentist appointment. Help others, but don't deny your own needs.

Tuesday, October 28 (Moon into Capricorn, 6:04 a.m.)   It's a number 4 day. Persevere to get things done today. Don't get sloppy. It's a time for hard work and fulfilling obligations. Put off any impulse to wander off task. It's not a good day for romance. You're building a foundation for the future.

Wednesday, October 29 (Moon in Capricorn)   The moon is in your seventh house today. Cooperation is highlighted. Don't make waves; just go with the flow. Loved ones and partners are more important than usual. A contract could play a role.

Thursday, October 30 (Moon into Aquarius, 9:52 a.m.)   Service to others is the theme of the day. You offer advice and support. Do a good deed for someone. An adjustment in your domestic life may be necessary now. You can be touchy and tend to avoid direct confrontations, Cancer. You can also be somewhat manipulative.

Friday, October 31 (Moon in Aquarius)   The moon is in your eighth house today. An interest in mystical matters plays a role in your day. You could be considering the possibility of reincarnation or examining what others say about life after death. You feel a connection with the other side.

NOVEMBER 2014

Saturday, November 1 (Moon in Pisces)   The moon is in your ninth house today, the home of higher learning. You're full of ideas now on matters such as philosophy or religion, the law or publishing. You also have a strong interest in foreign travel or a foreign nation. It's a good time to look at the big picture. Break away from your routine or the usual way you think about things.

Sunday, November 2—Daylight Saving Time Ends (Moon in Pisces)   Under the influence of the Pisces moon, you imagination is highlighted. You respond emotionally to whatever is happening now. Keep track of your dreams, including your daydreams. Ideas are ripe. You can tap deeply into the collective unconscious for inspiration. It's a day for deep healing.

Monday, November 3 (Moon into Aries, 1:54 p.m.) Look beneath the surface for the reasons others are shifting their points of view. But don't make any final decisions on what you uncover until tomorrow. Express your desires, but avoid self-deception. Maintain your emotional balance. Your challenge today is to be independent without feeling isolated. Avoid confusion and conflicts.

Tuesday, November 4 (Moon in Aries)   With the moon in your tenth house today, professional concerns are the focus. You celebrate your newfound prominence. Your prestige is elevated, especially through a promotion or raise. Your life is more public today. You're more emotional and warm toward coworkers.

Wednesday, November 5 (Moon into Taurus, 4:34 p.m.)   It's a number 9 day. Complete a project, and make room for something new. Visualize for the future. Set your goals, then make them so. Strive for universal appeal, but stay grounded. You're up to the challenge.

Thursday, November 6 (Moon in Taurus)   There's a full moon in your eleventh house today. You gain insight related to friends and associates. Your wishes and dreams play an important role. With Mars and Pluto forming beneficial angles, you're in the driver's seat. In spite of power plays taking place around you, you see the way ahead.

Friday, November 7 (Moon into Gemini, 8:45 p.m.) It's a number 2 day for you, Cancer, and that means cooperation is highlighted. Use your intuition to get a sense of your day. Be kind and nurturing. Show your appreciation to others. A new relationship could be developing.

Saturday, November 8 (Moon in Gemini)   Mercury moves into your fifth house today. You express yourself dramatically, either in speech or writing. You're mentally stimulated now and extremely competitive. You communicate well about a creative project or when dealing with children. You take a somewhat cool, analytical look at love.

Sunday, November 9 (Moon in Gemini)   The moon is in your twelfth house today. It's a good day to withdraw and work behind the scenes. It's best to hide your emotions and moodiness. Avoid stubbornness and any self-destructive behavior. Things concerning the past and your childhood play a role.

Monday, November 10 (Moon into Cancer, 3:39 a.m.) Change and variety are highlighted now. Release old structures; get a new point of view. It's a good time to pursue self-employment. You're courageous and adaptable, versatile and changeable. Think freedom, no restrictions.

Tuesday, November 11 (Moon in Cancer) The moon is in your first house today. You're sensitive to other people's feelings. You may feel moody one moment, happy the next, then withdrawn and sad. It's all about your emotional self. You tend to change your plans or procrastinate now, Cancer. Your feelings tend to fluctuate by the moment.

Wednesday, November 12 (Moon into Leo, 1:45 p.m.) It's a number 7 day, and you're getting very analytical, Cancer. You're looking into a mystery, digging deep for answers. Be aware of decisions made behind closed doors. Work on your own and gather information, but don't make any absolute decisions until tomorrow.

Thursday, November 13 (Moon in Leo) The moon is in your second house today. You feel best when surrounded by familiar objects. It's not the objects themselves that are important, but the feelings and memories you associate with them. Put off making any major purchases for a couple of days. Look at your priorities in handling your income.

Friday, November 14 (Moon in Leo) Under the influence of the Leo moon, your feelings are more intense than usual today, and there's high drama in the air as security becomes an important issue for you. Your sense of duty and obligation can affect your feelings about shared belongings. Matters of sex, death and rebirth, rituals, and relationships emerge now.

Saturday, November 15 (Moon into Virgo, 2:09 a.m.) Neptune goes direct in your ninth house today. You'll become more intuitive in the coming months and also more sensitive. You'll also be more comfortable proceeding with plans for higher education or long-distance travel. You start to take a closer look at a foreign land. A foreign-born person could play a role.

Sunday, November 16 (Moon in Virgo) Venus moves into your sixth house today. Your health picture improves over the next three weeks. In addition, your relationship with coworkers is enhanced. You are aligned mentally and emotionally. You could be helping others in the workplace, and that enhances your connection with them. Whatever happens, it'll be a positive experience.

Monday, November 17 (Moon into Libra, 2:31 p.m.) It's a number 3 day. You're innovative and creative and communicate well. You can influence people now with your upbeat attitude. Your artistic talents are highlighted. Ease up on your routines, and spread your good news. Your charm and wit are appreciated. Remain flexible.

Tuesday, November 18 (Moon in Libra) The moon is in your fourth house today. It's a good day to spend some time on a home-repair project and be with your family and loved ones. You're dealing with the foundations of who you are.

Wednesday, November 19 (Moon in Libra) Under the influence of the Libra moon, romance is highlighted. Relationship issues figure prominently in your day. It's a great day to schedule an adventurous encounter with your significant other. You're also looking for balance as you fine-tune a love relationship. Compassion is highlighted.

Thursday, November 20 (Moon into Scorpio, 12:32 a.m.) You're busy helping others today. You're sensitive and nurturing, Cancer. You offer advice and support. Be sympathetic and kind, generous and tolerant. Focus on making people happy. Diplomacy wins the way.

Friday, November 21 (Moon in Scorpio) The moon is in your fifth house today. Romance and sex for pleasure are highlighted. Your emotions tend to overpower your intellect now, and you're emotionally in touch with your creative side. You feel strongly attached to loved ones, particularly children.

Saturday, November 22 (Moon into Sagittarius, 7:20 a.m.) There's a new moon in your sixth house today. An opportunity comes your way as a result of your hard work. You improve, edit, and refine the work of others, and you're rewarded for it. Attend to details related to your health. Make a doctor or dentist appointment. Your personal health occupies your attention now.

Sunday, November 23 (Moon in Sagittarius)   Under the influence of the Sag moon, you see the big picture today, not just the details. You're restless and looking for a way to expand whatever you're doing, especially if it relates to travel or higher education. Worldviews are emphasized. Don't limit yourself. Keep track of your dreams, including your daydreams. Ideas are ripe.

Monday, November 24 (Moon into Capricorn, 11:32 a.m.)   It's a number 1 day, and you're at the top of your cycle again. Get out and meet new people, have new experiences, do something you've never done before. You're inventive and make connections that others overlook. You get a fresh start, a new beginning. Trust your hunches.

Tuesday, November 25 (Moon in Capricorn)   The moon is in your seventh house today. You feel a strong desire to work with a partner now. You don't feel complete unless you and your partner or spouse are in tune. Avoid conflicts; go with the flow.

Wednesday, November 26 (Moon into Aquarius, 2:23 p.m.)   Have fun today in preparation for tomorrow's discipline and focus. Take time to relax, enjoy yourself, recharge your batteries. Your charm and wit are appreciated.

Thursday, November 27 (Moon in Aquarius)   The moon is in your eighth house today. You can expect high emotions regarding a troubling matter, especially if it deals with shared belongings. You dig deep, seeking the details. Your mind is active, and you ask a lot of questions. A mortgage, insurance, or investments could play a role. Alternately, you could get into a heated discussion about a metaphysical subject, such as life after death.

Friday, November 28 (Moon into Pisces, 5:04 p.m.) It's a number 5 day. That means you're open to change and variety, and you desire to loosen any restrictions today. You're willing to take a risk and experiment. Variety is the spice of life, and change is good. Think outside the box.

Saturday, November 29 (Moon in Pisces) The moon is in your ninth house today. You're a dreamer and thinker. You may feel a need to get away now, a break from the usual routine. You yearn for a new experience. It's a good time to plan a long trip or sign up for a workshop or seminar.

Sunday, November 30 (Moon into Aries, 8:15 p.m.) It's a number 7 day. You pursue a mystery. Gather information, but don't make any absolute decisions until tomorrow. Go with the flow. Maintain emotional balance, and avoid confusion and conflict.

DECEMBER 2014

Monday, December 1 (Moon in Aries) The moon is in your tenth house today. Focus on your professional concerns as the week begins. You could be dealing with bosses and others in power. You can be more responsive to the needs and moods of others around you now. You keep everyone grounded, Cancer. But make sure you stay in balance yourself. A word of caution: An office romance could be dangerous.

Tuesday, December 2 (Moon in Aries)   Under the influence of the Aries moon, you can put a lot of energy into starting something new. It's a great time for initiating projects, launching new ideas, or brainstorming. Be careful not to act recklessly. Cancer and Scorpio play a role in your day.

Wednesday, December 3 (Moon into Taurus, 12:16 a.m.)   It's a number 8 day, your power day. You can go far with your plans and achieve financial success. You're playing with power today, so be careful not to hurt others. Open your mind to a new approach that could bring in big bucks.

Thursday, December 4 (Moon in Taurus)   Mars moves into your eighth house today and stays that way until January 12. Your experiences are more intense than usual. Your convictions are strong, and you can sway others with their power. You're aggressive in your pursuit of travel plans or higher education.

Friday, December 5 (Moon into Gemini, 5:29 a.m.) It's a number 1 day. You're at the top of your cycle. Trust your hunches today. You get a fresh start, a new beginning. You're inventive and make connections that others overlook.

Saturday, December 6 (Moon in Gemini)   There's a full moon in your twelfth house today, and that means you gain insight related to a matter from the past that has come to your attention. Meanwhile, Uranus forms a beneficial angle, suggesting that unexpected events related to a matter that you've been keeping secret work to your benefit. Your unconscious mind is busy. You're intuitive and can recall your dreams. With Jupiter in your favor now, you can expand whatever you're doing, especially if you're willing to work behind the scenes.

Sunday, December 7 (Moon into Cancer, 12:35 p.m.) It's a number 3 day, and everything eases up. The intensity you've been feeling evaporates. Be happy, positive, upbeat. Your attitude determines everything now. You're well liked and receive a social invitation. Your charm and wit are appreciated. Spend time in conversation, or get involved with a hobby.

Monday, December 8 (Moon in Cancer)   Jupiter goes retrograde in your second house today and stays that way until April 8. You could face some delays and misunderstandings related to finances. Try to keep control of your emotions when dealing with money matters. Look at your priorities in handling your income.

Tuesday, December 9 (Moon into Leo, 10:15 p.m.) Promote new ideas; follow your curiosity. Freedom of thought and action is key. You're versatile and changeable today. You can overcome obstacles with ease. Take risks; experiment.

Wednesday, December 10 (Moon in Leo)   Venus moves into your seventh house today, where it stays until January 4. A marriage or partnership takes on new importance. You prosper through a relationship, especially if you do your part in making it work. A romance flourishes.

Thursday, December 11 (Moon in Leo) The moon is in your second house today, Cancer. So it's a good day for dealing with money issues. Pay what you owe and collect what others owe you. You equate your financial assets with emotional security. Look at your priorities in handling your income.

Friday, December 12 (Moon into Virgo, 10:20 a.m.) Offer your advice and support. Do a good deed for someone. Be generous and tolerant. Diplomacy wins the way. An adjustment in your domestic life works out for the best. Be helpful, but dance to your own tune.

Saturday, December 13 (Moon in Virgo) You'll probably be running around today, taking care of chores in your everyday world. You could hear from a sibling, other relative, or neighbor, and if so you can expect an invitation. Control your emotions when expressing any opinions, especially on matters related to the past.

Sunday, December 14 (Moon into Libra, 11:05 p.m.) It's a number 1 day. Don't be afraid to turn in a new direction. Be independent and creative. You get a fresh start, a new beginning. You're inventive and make connections that others overlook.

Monday, December 15 (Moon in Libra) The moon is in your fourth house today. It's a good day to work on a home-repair project. Spend time with your family and loved ones. You're dealing with the foundations of who you are. Keep your goals in mind; follow your ideas. Be tenacious.

Tuesday, December 16 (Moon in Libra)   Mercury moves into your eighth house today, where it stays until January 5. As yesterday, you're on top of your game. You make use of your mind to explore deeper issues, a mystery that might be haunting you. Joint resources play a lead role in your day, and you could deal with taxes, insurance, or an inheritance.

Wednesday, December 17 (Moon into Scorpio, 9:52 a.m.)   It's a number 4 day. Persevere to get things done today. Take care of details, and don't get sloppy. Revise, rewrite. Be methodical and thorough, and control your impulses. Fulfill your obligations. You're building foundations for an outlet for your creativity. You tend to exhibit some perfectionist details.

Thursday, December 18 (Moon in Scorpio)   With the moon in your fifth house today, your emotions tend to overpower your intellect. It's a good day to take a chance, experiment. Be yourself; be emotionally honest. In love there's greater emotional depth to a relationship now.

Friday, December 19 (Moon into Sagittarius, 4:56 p.m.)   It's a number 6 day. Service to others is the theme of the day. You offer advice and support. Be sympathetic and kind, generous and tolerant. Focus on making people happy. Diplomacy wins the way.

Saturday, December 20 (Moon in Sagittarius)
The moon is in your sixth house today. It's a service day. You're the one others go to for help. Do what you can, but don't deny your own needs. Attend to details related to your health, Cancer. Make a doctor or dentist appointment.

Sunday, December 21 (Moon into Capricorn, 8:26 p.m.)   There's a new moon in your seventh house today. That means your interest turns to partnerships. You and a partner could get an opportunity for a new contract. Meanwhile, with Uranus going direct in your tenth house, you could get a boost in prestige related to your profession.

Monday, December 22 (Moon in Capricorn)   Yesterday's energy flows into your Monday as you feel a strong desire to work with a partner. You don't feel complete unless you and your partner or spouse are in tune. Avoid conflicts now. Go with the flow.

Tuesday, December 23 (Moon into Aquarius, 9:53 p.m.)   Saturn enters your sixth house today, where it stays for two and a half years. That means issues could arise over the coming months related to the workplace. You also could face difficulties in dealing with fellow workers. Keep close tabs on your emotions, especially when talking about relationship issues that you want to resolve.

Wednesday, December 24 (Moon in Aquarius)
With the moon in your eighth house today, your experiences are more intense than usual, especially related

to matters affecting shared property or resources. Security is an important issue with you right now. You also have a strong sense of duty and feel obligated to fulfill your promises.

Thursday, December 25 (Moon into Pisces, 11:08 p.m.)   It's a number 3 day. You're innovative and creative and communicate well. You can influence people now with your upbeat attitude. Ease up on your routines, and spread your good news. Your charm and wit are appreciated. Remain flexible. Merry Christmas!

Friday, December 26 (Moon in Pisces)   The moon is in your ninth house today. Your individuality is stressed. You're dealing with new ideas, new options, originality. Your visionary abilities are heightened. Your mind is active, and you yearn for new experiences, a break from the routine. Help others, but dance to your own tune.

Saturday, December 27 (Moon in Pisces)   Under the influence of the Pisces moon, your imagination is highlighted. You respond emotionally to whatever is happening. Keep track of your dreams, including your daydreams. Ideas are ripe. You can tap deeply into the collective unconscious for inspiration. It's a day for deep healing.

Sunday, December 28 (Moon into Aries, 1:36 a.m.) It's a number 6 day, a service day. Be diplomatic, especially with someone who is giving you trouble. Do a good deed. Visit someone who is ill or in need of help.

Be sympathetic, kind, and compassionate, but avoid scattering your energies.

Monday, December 29 (Moon in Aries) The moon is in your tenth house today. Professional concerns are the focus of the day. You celebrate your newfound prominence. Your prestige is elevated, especially through a promotion or raise. Your life is more public. You're more emotional and warm toward coworkers.

Tuesday, December 30 (Moon into Taurus, 5:57 a.m.) It's a number 8 day, a good day to buy a lotto ticket. It's your power day, your day to play it your way. You can go far with your plans and achieve financial success. Unexpected money comes your way.

Wednesday, December 31 (Moon in Taurus) The moon is in your eleventh house today. You get along well with friends, who surprise you with their offers of assistance. You work well with a group. Follow your wishes and dreams, and make sure that they are still an expression of who you are.

HAPPY NEW YEAR!

SYDNEY OMARR

Born on August 5, 1926, in Philadelphia, Pennsylvania, **Sydney Omarr** was the only person ever given full-time duty in the U.S. Army as an astrologer. He is regarded as the most erudite astrologer of the twentieth century and the best known, through his syndicated column and his radio and television programs (he was Merv Griffin's "resident astrologer"). Omarr has been called the most "knowledgeable astrologer since Evangeline Adams." His forecasts of Nixon's downfall, the end of World War II in mid-August of 1945, the assassination of John F. Kennedy, Roosevelt's election to a fourth term and his death in office . . . these and many others are on the record and quoted enough to be considered "legendary."

ABOUT THE SERIES

This is one of a series of twelve *Sydney Omarr®
Day-by-Day Astrological Guides* for the signs of
2014. For questions and comments about the
book, go to www.sydneyomarr.blogspot.com.